中国地质调查成果 CGS 2017-086
湖北省学术著作出版专项资金资助项目

中国重要经济区和城市群地质环境图集

长江经济带 国土资源与重大地质问题图集

ATLAS OF LAND RESOURCES AND MOMENTOUS GEOLOGICAL PROBLEMS IN YANGTZE RIVER ECONOMIC ZONE

中国地质调查局 编著

内 容 简 介

《长江经济带国土资源与重大地质问题图集》是国土资源部中国地质调查局"长江经济带地质环境综合调查工程"和"长三角南京-上海-温州城镇规划区1∶5万环境地质调查项目"的研究成果之一。图集收集了长江经济带以往地学研究成果以及近年来的地质调查成果，涵盖了基础地质、水文地质、工程地质、环境地质、能源与矿产地质、海洋地质和地球化学等专业。图集内容包括长江经济带城镇与基础设施规划需要关注的重大地质问题、产业发展规划布局需要考虑的能源与资源潜力、耕地保护和管理需要重视的土地质量地球化学背景、国土开发与生态环境保护需要重视的资源环境状况、长江三角洲海岸带地区的国土资源与环境条件5个方面，是长江经济带绿色生态廊道打造、立体交通走廊建设、产业转型升级、新型城镇化建设和脱贫攻坚等重要基础资料。

本图集可供从事基础地质、水文地质、工程地质、环境地质、能源与矿产地质、海洋地质和地球化学等专业的教学和科研人员以及制定相关政策的政府部门参考使用。

图书在版编目（CIP）数据

长江经济带国土资源与重大地质问题图集/中国地质调查局编著.—武汉:中国地质大学出版社，2018.11
（中国重要经济区和城市群地质环境图集）
ISBN 978-7-5625-4266-7

Ⅰ.①长…
Ⅱ.①中…
Ⅲ.①长江经济带-国土资源-图集②长江经济带-地质环境-图集
Ⅳ.①F129.9-54②X141-54

中国版本图书馆CIP数据核字（2018）第079986号
审图号：GS（2018）6040号

长江经济带国土资源与重大地质问题图集		中国地质调查局 编著
责任编辑：胡珞兰 王凤林	选题策划：唐然坤 毕克成	责任校对：徐蕾蕾
出版发行：中国地质大学出版社（武汉市洪山区鲁磨路388号）		邮政编码：430074
电　　话：（027）67883511	传　　真：67883580	Email:cbb @ cug.edu.cn
经　　销：全国新华书店		http://cugp.cug.edu.cn
开本：400毫米×275毫米 1/8		字数：333千字　印张：10.5
版次：2018年11月第1版		印次：2018年11月第1次印刷
印刷：中煤地西安地图制印有限公司		印数：1—500册
ISBN 978-7-5625-4266-7		定价：280.00元

如有印装质量问题请与印刷厂联系调换

《长江经济带国土资源与重大地质问题图集》
编 委 会

编辑委员会

主　　任	郝爱兵								
副 主 编	李基宏	文冬光	张训华	邢卫国	郭坤一	何庆成	邢光福	苗培森	张旺池	张永双
	齐先茂	张永波	张作晨	孙晓明	龙宝林	张生辉	叶建良	张海啟	任收麦	高延光
	石　森	张智勇	蔺志永	刘凤山	张先林	黄克蓉	邱鸿坤	龚健勇	龚　勇	熊保成
	王礼光	鲁豫川	蒋　俊	赵福平	任　坚	贾克敬				
编　　委	（按姓氏笔画排序）								
	冯小铭	陈立德	倪化勇	林良俊	金维群	姜　义	姜月华	胡秋韵	石菊松	黄长生
	葛伟亚	黎清华	李明辉	陈国光	程光华	朱锦旗	严学新	姚洪华	龚日详	殷世新
	战双庆	朱省峰	徐贵来	杨明银	黄建中	颜　春	楼法生	祝立人	赵　春	李进财
	杨胜元									

执行编辑委员会

主　　编	姜月华	林良俊								
副 主 编	周权平	葛伟亚	苏晶文	陈立德	倪化勇	祁　帆	班宜忠	李　云	张泰丽	印　萍
	雷明堂	李　媛	成杭新	谭成轩	尹成明	贾学天	赵建康	王寒梅	于　军	陈忠大
	程　霞	彭玉怀	王龙平	李建设	刘建东	肖尚德	黄革非	赵德君	孙四权	魏昌利
	王　磊	张建江	刘　喜	李明辉	尹国胜	林清龙	李瑞敏	王贵玲	贾克敬	
编　　委	田福金	邢怀学	贾军元	周　迅	黄金玉	叶念军	李云峰	刘红樱	龚建师	张　明
	杨　辉	梁晓红	高天山	许乃政	杨祝良	侯莉莉	朱春芳	周锴锷	杨国强	刘　林

	常晓军	孙　强	魏　峰	李　亮	伍剑波	王赫生	叶永红	杨　洋	余　成	雷　廷
	张　庆	金　阳	彭　轲	邵长生	何　军	齐　信	曾春芳	李金柱	史玉金	李　晓
	陆　华	理继红	王光亚	黄敬军	张达政	张雨顺	黎　伟	陈大平	余俊英	方　正
	徐玉琳	龚绪龙	武建强	刘建东	王贵林	徐敏成	胡光明	郑万模	李明辉	曲雪妍
	张森琦	戴建玲	杨齐青	荆继红	李运怀	李志刚	李书涛	范　毅	汪　凡	杨　曼
	罗　维	孟　伟	朱广毅	朱悦彰	周国华	王东辉	李旭峰	李长顺	廖　维	李鸿雁
	梁　波	韦玉婷	胥　良	陈绪钰	徐如阁	田　凯	杨　春	罗宇浩	鲍丽然	孙　勇
	肖志坚	陈建保	杨树云	张　贵	罗炳佳	张天友	鲍志言	饶　志	徐定芳	
制　图	周权平	苏晶文	黄金玉	邢怀学	周　迅	李　云	刘红樱	杨国强	白建平	
翻　译	朱意萍	苏晶文								
地图设计	高晓梅	植忠红								
地图制版	张　魏	吕　艳	马君睿	万　波	董米茹	吴　瑶	郑欣媛	高宝丽		

Atlas of Land Resources and Momentous Geological Problems in Yangtze River Economic Zone Editorial Committee

Editorial Committee

Chief Editor　　Hao Aibing

Associate Editor

Li Jihong	Wen Dongguang	Zhang Xunhua	Xing Weiguo	Guo Kunyi	He Qingcheng	Xing Guangfu
Miao Peisen	Zhang Wangchi	Zhang Yongshuang	Qi Xianmao	Zhang Yongbo	Zhang Zuochen	Sun Xiaoming
Long Baolin	Zhang Shenghui	Ye Jianliang	Zhang Haiqi	Ren Shoumai	Gao Yanguang	Shi Sen
Zhang Zhiyong	Lin Zhiyong	Liu Fengshan	Zhang Xianlin	Huang Kerong	Qiu Hongkun	Gong Jianyong
Gong Yong	Xiong Baocheng	Wang Liguang	Lu Yuchuan	Jiang Jun	Zhao Fuping	Ren Jian
Jia Kejing						

Editor　　(In Chinese-character stroke order)

Feng Xiaoming	Chen Lide	Ni Huayong	Lin Liangjun	Jin Weiqun	Jiang Yi	Jiang Yuehua
Hu Qiuyun	Shi Jusong	Huang Changsheng	Ge Weiya	Li Qinghua	Li Minghui	Chen Guoguang
Cheng Guanghua	Zhu Jinqi	Yan Xuexin	Yao Honghua	Gong Rixiang	Yin Shixin	Zhan Shuangqing
Zhu Shengfeng	Xu Guilai	Yang Mingyin	Huang Jianzhong	Yan Chun	Lou Fasheng	Zhu Liren
Zhao Chun	Li Jincai	Yang Shengyuan				

Executive Editorial Committee

Chief Editor　　Jiang Yuehua　　Lin Liangjun

Associate Editor

Zhou Quanping	Ge Weiya	Su Jinwen	Chen Lide	Ni Huayong	Qi Fan	Ban Yizhong
Li Yun	Zhang Taili	Yin Ping	Lei Mingtang	Li Yuan	Cheng Hangxin	Tan Zhengxuan
Yin Chengming	Jia Xuetian	Zhao Jiankang	Wang Hanmei	Yu Jun	Chen Zhongda	Cheng Xia
Peng Yuhuai	Wang Longping	Li Jianshe	Liu Jiandong	Xiao Shangde	Huang Gefei	Zhao Dejun
Sun Siquan	Wei Changli	Wang Lei	Zhang Jianjiang	Liu Xi	Li Minghui	Yin Guosheng
Lin Qinglong	Li Ruimin	Wang Guiling	Jia Kejing			

Member　　(In Chinese-character stroke order)

Tian Fujin	Xing Huaixue	Jia Junyuan	Zhou Xun	Huang Jinyu	Ye Nianjun	Li Yunfeng
Liu Hongying	Gong Jianshi	Zhang Ming	Yang Hui	Liang Xiaohong	Gao Tianshan	Xu Naizheng

Yang Zhuliang	Hou Lili	Zhu Chunfang	Zhou Kaie	Yang Guoqiang	Liu Lin	Chang Xiaojun
Sun Qiang	Wei Feng	Li Liang	Wu Jianbo	Wang Hesheng	Ye Yonghong	Yang Yang
Yu Cheng	Lei Ting	Zhang Qing	Jin Yang	Peng Ke	Shao Changsheng	He Jun
Qi Xin	Zeng Chunfang	Li Jinzhu	Shi Yujin	Li Xiao	Lu Hua	Li Jihong
Wang Guangya	Huang Jingjun	Zhang Dazheng	Zhang Yushun	Li Wei	Chen Daping	Yu Junying
Fang Zheng	Xu Yulin	Gong Xulong	Wu Jianqiang	Liu Jiandong	Wang Guilin	Xu Mincheng
Hu Guangming	Zheng Wanmo	Li Minghui	Qu Xueyan	Zhang Senqi	Dai Jianling	Yang Qiqing
Jing Jihong	Li Yunhuai	Li Zhigang	Li Shutao	Fan Yi	Wang Fan	Yang Man
Luo Wei	Meng Wei	Zhu Guangyi	Zhu Yuezhang	Zhou Guohua	Wang Donghui	Li Xufeng
Li Changshun	Liao Wei	Li Hongyan	Liang Bo	Wei Yuting	Xu Liang	Chen Xuyu
Xu Ruge	Tian Kai	Yang Chun	Luo Yuhao	Bao Liran	Sun Yong	Xiao Zhijian
Chen Jianbao	Yang Shuyun	Zhang Gui	Luo Bingjia	Zhang Tianyou	Bao Zhiyan	Rao Zhi
Xu Dingfang						

Cartographer Zhou Quanping   Su Jingwen   Huang Jinyu   Xing Huaixue   Zhou Xun   Li Yun
Liu Hongying   Yang Guoqiang   Bai Jinping

Translator Zhu Yiping   Su Jingwen

Map Design Gao Xiaomei   Zhi Zhonghong

Map Printing Zhang Wei   Lü Yan   Ma Junrui   Wan Bo   Dong Miru   Wu Yao   Zheng Xinyuan   Gao Baoli

前　言

长江经济带横跨我国东中西部11个省（市），面积约$205\times10^4 km^2$，人口和地区生产总值均超过全国的40%，是我国综合实力最强、战略支撑作用最大的区域之一。

长江经济带资源环境条件较为优越，承载能力良好，发展空间和潜力很大。耕地总面积$4\,511\times10^4 hm^2$（$1hm^2=0.01km^2$），占全国的33.4%。能源与矿产资源丰富，有8个国家级重点成矿带，天然气储量约占全国的28%，页岩气、地热资源开发潜力很大。水资源总量$11\,000\times10^8 m^3$，约占全国的35%。

由于自然地理和地质条件差异变化大，在强烈的人类活动影响下，上、中、下游地区分别产生了一些重大地质问题，需要引起高度关注。上游的重庆、四川、云南、贵州4省（市）崩塌、滑坡、泥石流地质灾害点多面广、高发频发；局部地壳稳定性差，活动断裂发育；中游的安徽、江西、湖南、湖北4省岩溶塌陷、湖泊生态退化、矿山环境问题突出；下游的上海、江苏、浙江3省（市）地面沉降、地裂缝、水土污染、海岸侵蚀淤积等地质问题较为严重。

长期以来，国土资源部门在长江经济带积极开展自然资源与环境的调查评价，系统获取了土地、矿产、能源、海洋、地下水、环境、灾害防治等方面的调查研究成果。以此为基础，编制了《长江经济带国土资源与重大地质问题图集》，从服务城镇与基础设施规划、产业发展规划布局、耕地保护和质量管理、国土开发与生态环境保护、海岸带开发与保护5个方面提出了建议，以期为长江经济带的区域协调发展和生态文明建设的先行示范提供基础信息与重要依据。

《长江经济带国土资源与重大地质问题图集》是由中国地质调查局负责组织，技术牵头单位为中国地质调查局南京地质调查中心，参加单位包括中国地质调查局武汉地质调查中心、中国地质调查局成都地质调查中心、中国地质环境监测院、中国土地勘测规划院、中国地质调查局天津地质调查中心、中国地质调查局水文地质环境地质调查中心、中国地质科学院水文地质环境地质研究所、中国地质科学院岩溶地质研究所、中国地质科学院地质力学研究所、中国地质调查局青岛海洋地质研究所、中国地质科学院地质研究所、中国国土资源航空物探遥感中心、中国地质调查局发展研究中心、全国地质资料馆，以及江苏、浙江、上海、安徽、江西、湖北、湖南、四川、重庆、云南、贵州11个省（市）国土资源厅（局）、地质矿产勘查开发局、地质调查院、地质环境监测总站等。图集的编制和出版得到了中国地质调查局钟自然局长、王研副局长、李金发副局长、王昆副局长和严光生总工程师的关心和指导，得到了中国地质调查局郝爱兵、文冬光、李基宏、石建省、金若时、姚华舟、徐学义、李文昌、马军、刘同良、徐勇、吴能友、侯增谦、韩子夜、张海啟、严兴华，中国土地勘测规划院高延利以及长江经济带11省（市）国土资源部门岑福康、刘聪、张金根、潘海滨、侯克常、徐振坤、李国清、周时洪、徐志文、王赤兵、李连举等领导的大力支持，同时，也得到了很多专家学者的指导和建议，在此一并表示衷心的感谢。由于编者水平有限，难免存在疏漏和不足，恳请读者赐教，以便修改完善。

编委会

2017年9月21日

Preface

The Yangtze River Economic Zone spans across 11 provinces and municipal cities from midwestern to eastern China with the coverage of $205×10^4 km^2$. Both its population and regional GDP account for more than 40% of the national total. It is one of the regions that have the most powerful overall strength and strategic supports in China.

With more advantageous resources and environment and good carrying capacity, the Yangtze River Economic Zone has huge potentiality for development. It covers a cultivated area of $4,511×10^4 hm^2$, accounting for 33.4% of national total. There is abundant energy mineral resources with 8 key national-level metallogenic belts and huge exploitation potentiality for shale gas and geothermal resources in the zone, where the natural gas reserve accounts for 28% of the national total. The total water resource reaches to $11,000×10^8 m^3$ accounting for 35% of the national total.

In view of distinct variations of natural geography and geological condition, some momentous geological problems have emerged in the regions along the Yangtze River due to influence of intense human activities, which should call for great concern. In Chongqing municipality, Sichuan, Yunnan and Guizhou Provinces of the River's upper reaches, with the poor stability of regional crustal and the active faults, collapses, landslides and debris flows are triggered frequently and widely. In Anhui, Jiangxi, Hunan and Hubei Provinces along the middle reaches, there are striking problems related to karst collapse, degradation of lake ecosystem and mining-related environmental problems. While Shanghai municipality, Jiangsu and Zhejiang Provinces in the lower reaches are confronting severe geological problems such as ground subsidence, ground fissure, water and soil contamination and coastal erosion and siltation.

Over many years, sectors of national land and resources at all levels have committed to the investigation and appraisal on natural resources and environment. Based on the output of the holistic research with respect of land, mineral resources, energy, ocean, groundwater, environment, geohazard prevention and control, we compiled the *Atlas of Land Resources and Momentous Geological Problems in Yangtze River Economic Zone* and made suggestions from five aspects, i.e. urban and infrastructural planning, layout of industrial development planning, cultivated land protection and quality control, national land exploitation and ecological environment protection, coastal area development and protection, aiming to provide the Yangtze River Economic Zone with elementary information and important reference for the regional coordinated development and the paradigm of ecological advancement.

Atlas of Land Resources and Momentous Geological Problems in Yangtze River Economic Zone was organized by China Geological Survey (CGS) with the technical leadership by Nanjing Center of CGS and the active participation by Wuhan Center of CGS, Chengdu Center of CGS, China Institute for Geoenvironmental Monitoring, Chinese Land Surveying and Planning Institute, Tianjin Center of CGS, Hydrogeological and Environmental Geological Survey of CGS, Institute of Hydrogeology and Environmental Geology of Chinese Academy of Geological Sciences (CAGS), Institute of Karst Geology of CAGS, Institute of Geomechanics of CAGS, Qingdao Institute of Marine Geology of CGS, Institute of Geology of CAGS, China Aero Geophysical Survey and Remote Sensing Center for Land and Resources, Development and Research Center of CGS, China Geological Library, as well as the departments and bureaus of land and resources, bureaus for geology and mineral resources exploration and development, institutes of geological survey, general stations of geological environmental monitoring in 11 provinces and municipalities including Jiangsu, Zhejiang, Shanghai, Anhui, Jiangxi, Hubei, Hunan, Sichuan, Chongqing, Yunnan and Guizhou. Dr. Zhong Ziran, the Vice Minister of Geological Survey, Ministry of Land and Resources of China, President of China Geological Survey, Vice President Dr. Wang Yan, Vice President Dr. Li Jinfa, Vice President Dr. Wang Kun and Chief Engineer Dr. Yan Guangsheng of China Geological Survey, All of the directors paid great attention and gave detailed instruction on the compilation and publication of the atlas, which also acquired strong support from Hao Aibing, Wen Dongguang, Li Jihong, Shi Jiansheng, Jin Ruoshi, Yao Huazhou, Xu Xueyi, Li Wenchang, Ma Jun, Liu Tongliang, Xu Yong, Wu Nengyou, Hou Zengqian, Han Ziye, Zhang Haiqi, Yan Xinghua from China Geological Survey, Gao Yanli from Chinese Land Surveying and Planning Institute, and Cen Fukang, Liu Cong, Zhang Jingen, Pan Haibin, Hou Kechang, Xu Zhenkun, Li Guoqing, Zhou Shihong, Xu Zhiwen, Wang Chibing, Li Lianju and other people from the departments of land and resources in 11 provinces and municipalities within the Yangtze River Economic Zone. At the same time, we have also received a lot of experts' and scholars' guidance and recommendations, and hereby express our heartfelt and sincere appreciation. Due to the limited level of editors' knowledge, it is inevitable that some omissions and deficiencies exist in the work, and we urge the readers to enlighten us for improvement.

Editorial Committee
2017/9/21

目 录

1 城镇与基础设施规划需要关注的重大地质问题
1.1 长江经济带城镇与重要基础设施规划建设地质适宜性图 ······ 2
1.2 沿长江港口建设适宜性分区图（江苏段） ······ 3
1.3 长江经济带城镇化地区分布图 ······ 4
1.4 长江经济带国土开发强度图 ······ 5
1.5 长江经济带地质灾害分布与易发程度分区图 ······ 6
1.6 长江经济带岩溶塌陷分布及危险性评价分区图 ······ 7
1.7 长江经济带活动断裂与区域地壳稳定性评价图 ······ 8
1.8 长三角经济区地面沉降与地裂缝现状图 ······ 9

2 产业发展规划布局需要考虑的能源与资源潜力
2.1 长江经济带能源矿产资源分布图 ······ 12
2.2 长江经济带地热资源分布图 ······ 13
2.3 长江经济带矿产资源开发利用图 ······ 14
2.4 长江经济带矿产资源潜力图 ······ 15
2.5 长江经济带金属矿产资源分布图 ······ 16
2.6 长江经济带非金属矿产资源分布图 ······ 17
2.7 长江经济带地下水资源分布图 ······ 18

3 耕地保护和管理需要重视的土地质量地球化学背景
3.1 长江经济带平原丘陵区绿色农产品产地适宜性分区图 ······ 20
3.2 长江经济带平原丘陵区土地有益元素综合分区图 ······ 21
3.3 长江经济带土壤类型图 ······ 22
3.4 长江经济带耕地分布图 ······ 23
3.5 长江经济带平原丘陵区土地环境质量综合分区图 ······ 24
3.6 长三角经济区平原土地质量地球化学分区图 ······ 25

4 国土开发与生态环境保护需要重视的资源环境状况
4.1 长江经济带地貌图 ······ 28
4.2 长江经济带国土分类保护区划图 ······ 29
4.3 长江经济带生态功能区划图 ······ 30
4.4 长江经济带生态用地分布图 ······ 31
4.5 长江经济带生态敏感区分布图 ······ 32
4.6 长江经济带重要湖泊湿地保护建议图 ······ 33
4.7 长三角经济区平原地下水污染状况图 ······ 34
4.8 长三角经济区平原地下水"三氮"污染状况图 ······ 35
4.9 长三角经济区平原地下水重金属、有机组分污染图 ······ 35
4.10 长江经济带二氧化碳地质储存适宜性分区图 ······ 36

5 长江三角洲海岸带地区的国土资源与环境条件
5.1 长三角经济区滩涂后备土地资源潜力图 ······ 38
5.2 长三角经济区海域矿产资源分布图 ······ 38
5.3 长三角经济区海域滨海湿地分布图 ······ 39
5.4 长三角经济区海域水深地形图 ······ 39

附 件
支撑服务长江经济带发展地质调查报告（2015年）——长江经济带建设需关注的四大有利资源环境条件和四个重大地质问题 ······ 40

附 图
附图1 长江经济带无重金属污染和富硒耕地分布图 ······ 42
附图2 长江经济带地热资源分布图 ······ 43
附图3 长江经济带活动断裂与地震分布图 ······ 44
附图4 长江经济带岩溶塌陷易发性评价图 ······ 45
附图5 长江经济带滑坡、崩塌、泥石流分布及易发性评价图 ······ 46
附图6 长江经济带高速铁路、过江通道及重大地质问题图 ······ 47
附图7 长江经济带城市群及主要城市分布图 ······ 48
附图8 长江经济带大型矿产资源基地分布图 ······ 49

附 表
附表1 长江经济带无重金属污染耕地和绿色富硒耕地分布 ······ 50
附表2 影响长江经济带过江通道建设的重大地质问题 ······ 50
附表3 长江经济带过江通道方式建议 ······ 50
附表4 长三角城市群地面沉降及其影响城市 ······ 50
附表5 长江中游城市群岩溶塌陷及其影响城市 ······ 51
附表6 成渝城市群主要地质问题及其影响城市 ······ 51
附表7 长江经济带大型矿产资源基地 ······ 51

英文对照说明 ······ 52

后记 ······ 68

地理底图图例

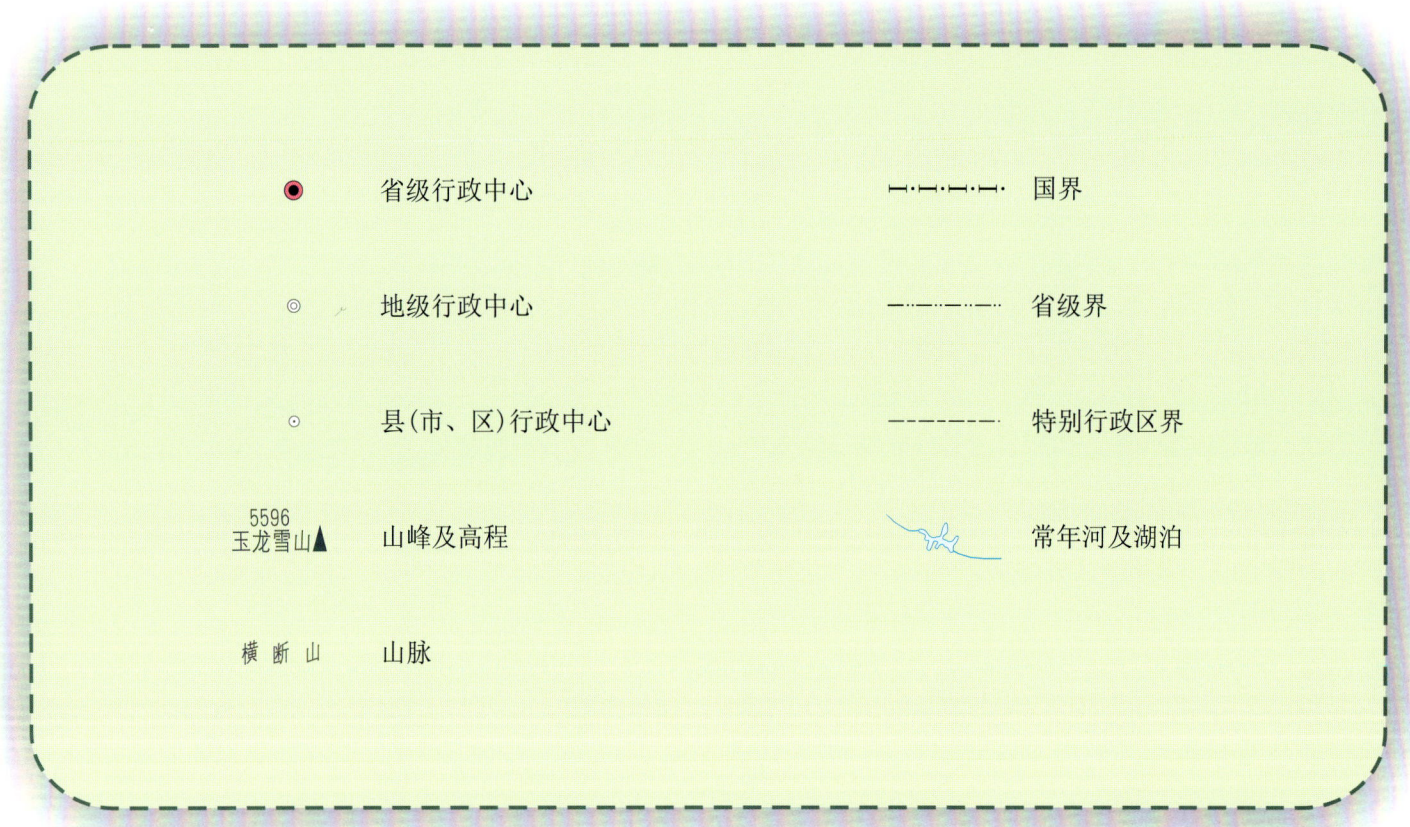

城镇与基础设施规划需要关注的重大地质问题

Momentous Geological Problems Needing Attention for Urban and Infrastructural Planning

1

1.1 长江经济带城镇与重要基础设施规划建设地质适宜性图
The Geological Suitability Map for Planning and Development of Urban and Important Infrastructure

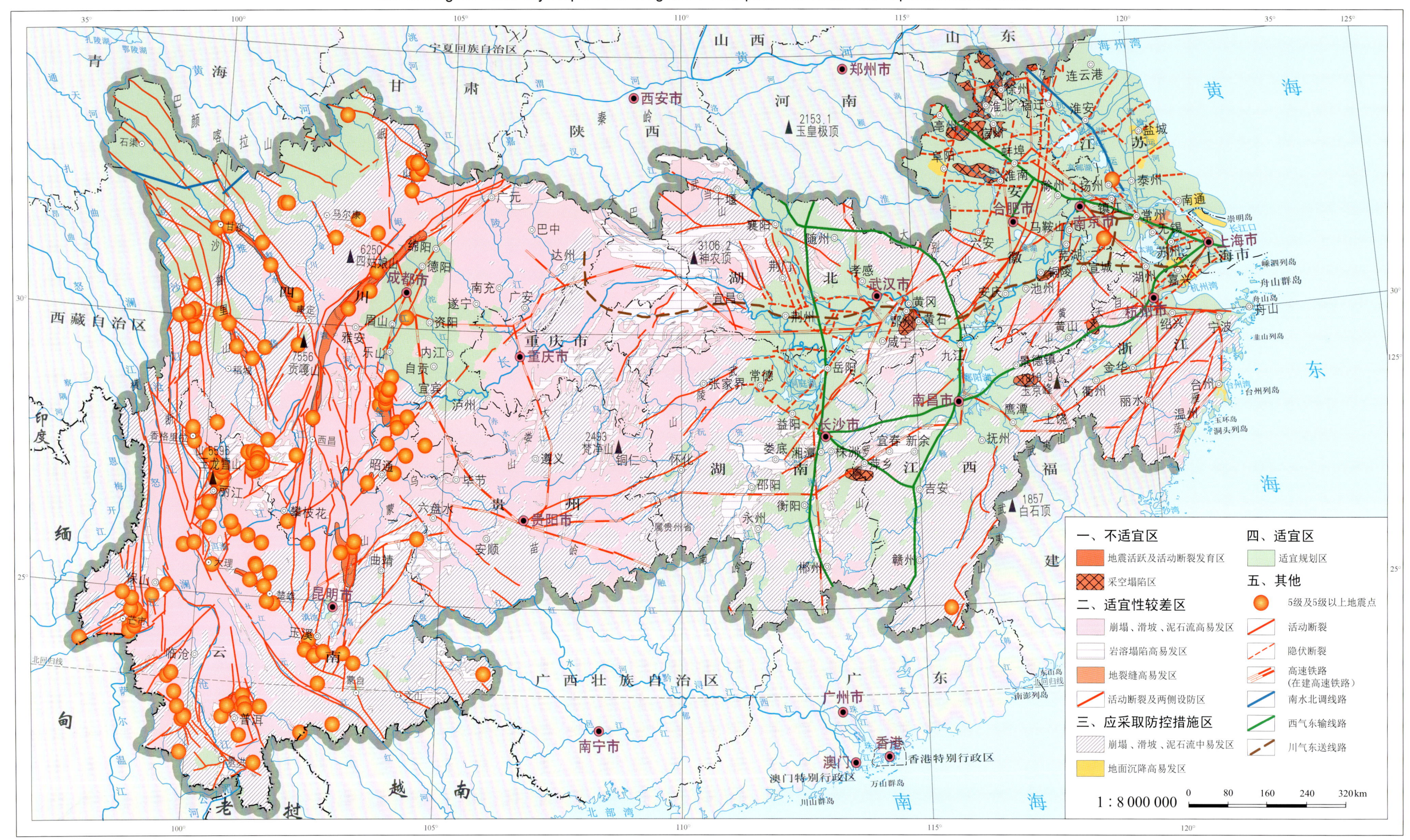

从地质安全考虑，长江经济带城镇与重要基础设施建设用地适宜性可分为4类。第一类是不适宜区，包括地震活跃（5级以上）和主要活动断裂两侧地区以及采矿造成的采空塌陷区；第二类是适宜性较差区，包括崩塌、滑坡、泥石流、岩溶塌陷、地裂缝高易发区及除不适宜区之外其他活动断裂带两侧；第三类是应采取防控措施区，包括崩塌、滑坡、泥石流地质灾害中易发区和由于人类活动造成的地面沉降高易发区；第四类是适宜区，为上述3类地区以外，目前尚未发现重大地质问题的地区。

1.2 沿长江港口建设适宜性分区图（江苏段）
The Suitability Zoning Map for Port Construction along the Yangtze River (Jiangsu Segment)

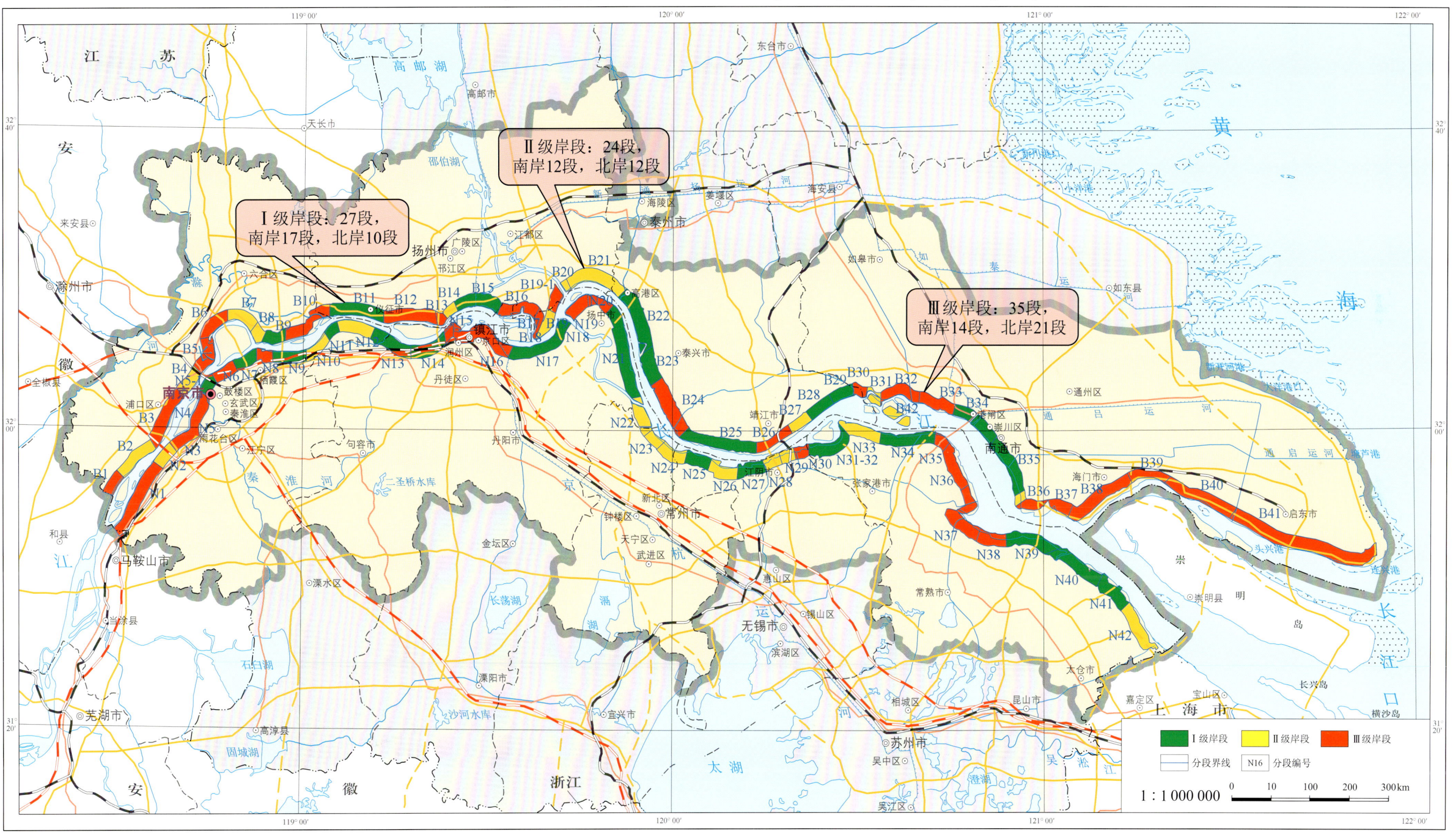

通过对不同岸段港口码头建设适宜性综合评价，按照其适宜性由好到差，将其分为Ⅰ、Ⅱ、Ⅲ三个等级。其中，Ⅰ级岸段表示港口码头建设适宜性好，Ⅱ级岸段表示适宜性较好，Ⅲ级岸段表示适宜性一般。评价结果表明，港口码头建设适宜性Ⅰ级岸段27段，Ⅱ级岸段24段，Ⅲ级岸段35段。其中，Ⅰ级岸段全部属于深水岸线，工程地质条件优良，航道宽度及通达性均满足建设万吨级及以上泊位的要求，为港口码头优先开发岸段，可以作为近期建设规划优先使用。

1.3 长江经济带城镇化地区分布图
The Distribution Map of Urbanization Area in the Yangtze River Economic Zone

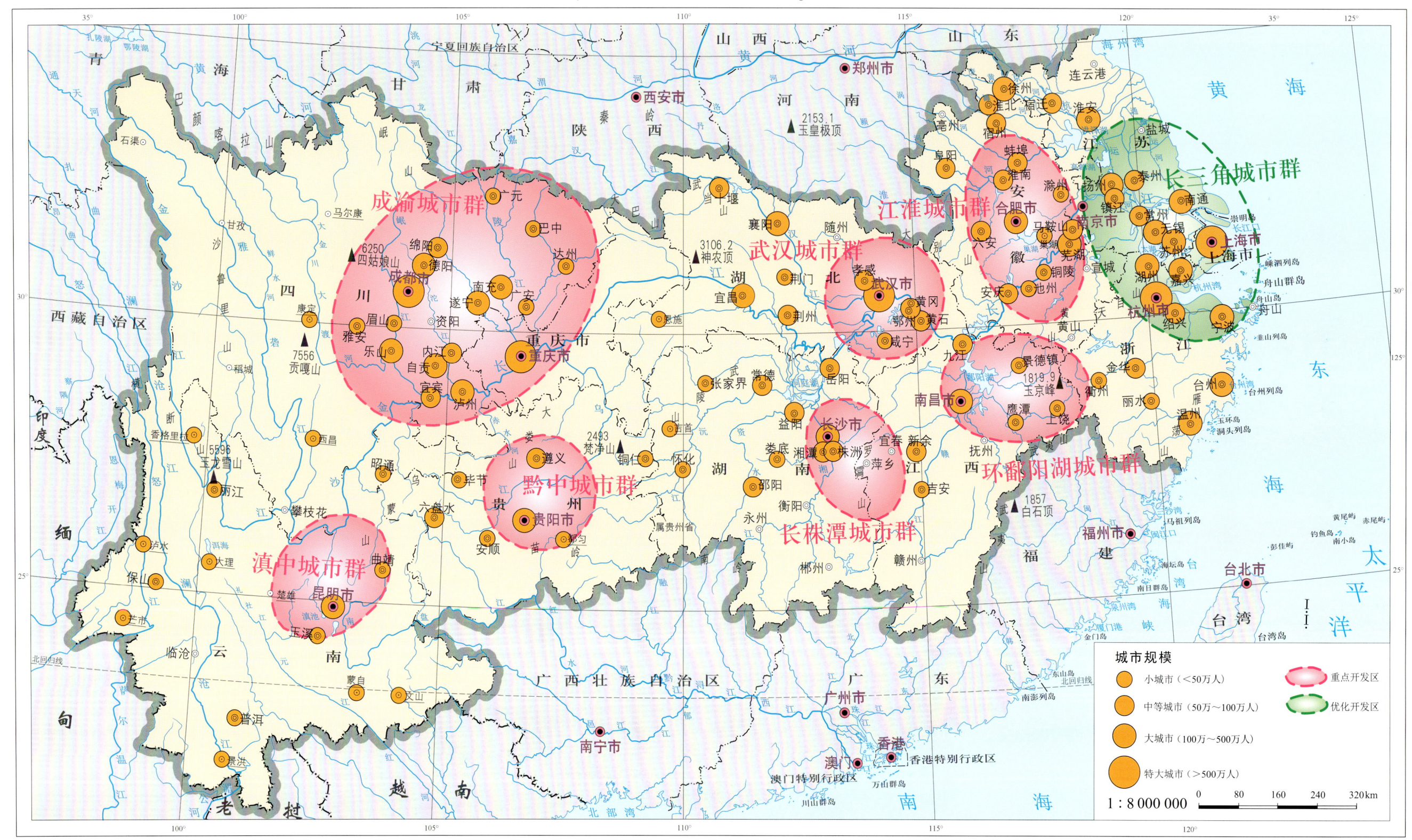

长江经济带主要城镇化地区（城市）指该区域内各种规模的主要城市所在地，具体包含了以下4种类型：①特大城市，指城区人口500万以上的城市，包括上海、杭州、南京、武汉、成都和重庆等长江经济带内各城市群的核心城市；②大城市，指城区人口在100万~500万之间的城市，包括如苏州、长沙、贵阳、温州、昆明等长江经济带内各省的中心城市；③中等城市，指城区人口在50万~100万之间的城市，如泰州、宜昌、孝感、常德、遵义、宁波、绵阳、邵阳等各省的重要城市；④小城市，指城区人口小于50万人的城市。

1.4 长江经济带国土开发强度图
The Development Intensity Map of the Country's Lands in the Yangtze River Economic Zone

长江经济带国土开发强度主要根据单个格网（1km×1km）内城镇工矿建设用地所占面积的比率获得。开发强度由弱到强依次分为0~20%、20%~40%、40%~60%、60%~80%、80%~100%。从整体来看，长江经济带建设用地开发强度整体呈现出东部较高、西部较低的趋势。长江三角洲区域的国土开发强度最高。开发强度与城市建设具有较高的一致性，以各省主要城市为核心的开发区域散布在长江经济带。

1.5 长江经济带地质灾害分布与易发程度分区图
The Distribution Map of Geohazards and Susceptablility Degree in the Yangtze River Economic Zone

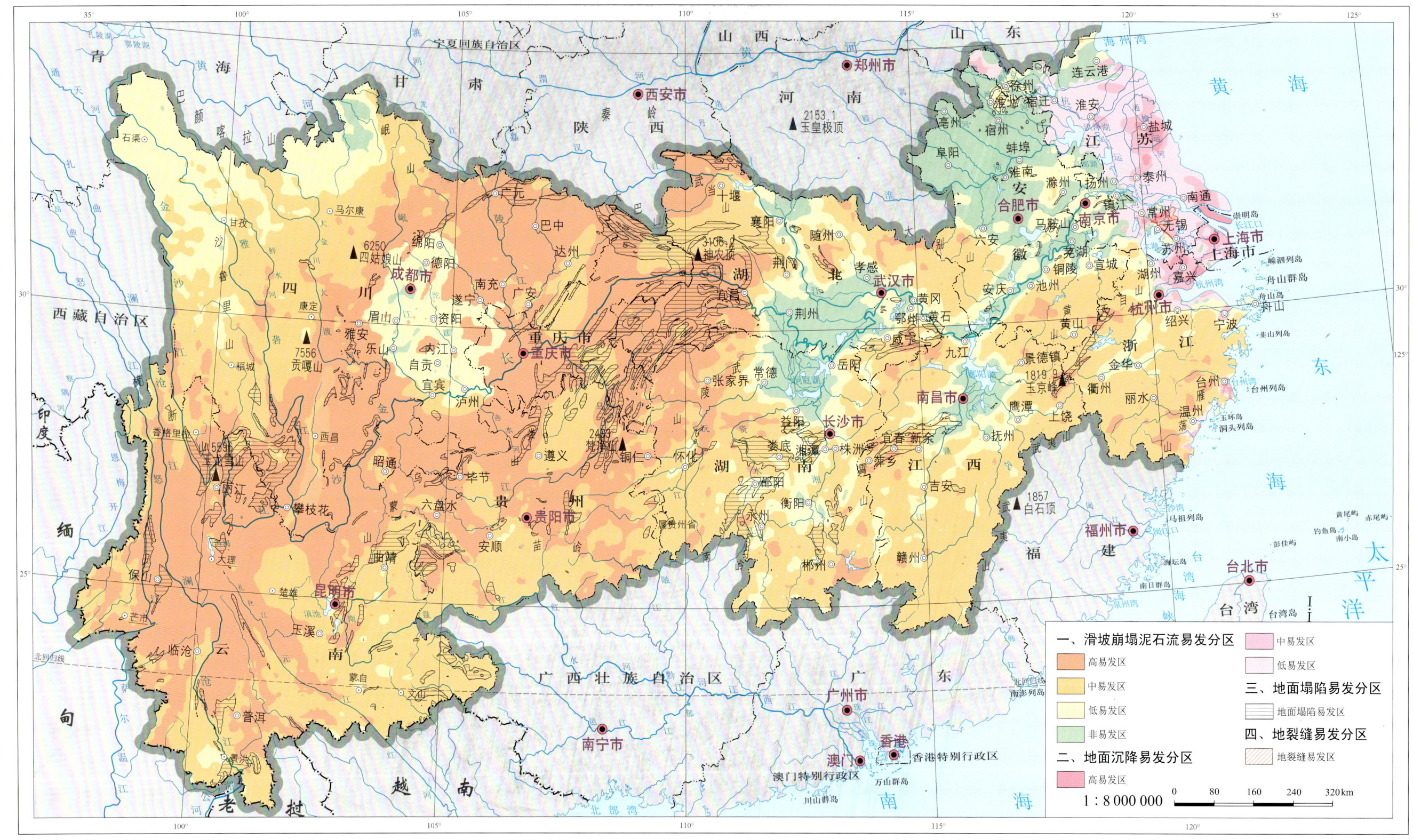

滑坡、崩塌、泥石流易发区：主要分布在怒江、澜沧江、金沙江三江汇流区，龙门山断裂带和鄂黔滇中山区。调查确认滑坡、崩塌、泥石流地质灾害及隐患点有106 760处。地面沉降与地裂缝易发区：主要分布于上海、江苏和杭嘉湖等地，高易发区面积为6 690.9 km²，沉降中心区最大沉降量达2.63 m。目前已发现20余处地裂缝灾害。地面塌陷易发区：调查确认地面塌陷5 323处，主要分布在重庆东部、武汉西部、贵州北部、云南东北部、湖南中部和徐淮地区，其中，高易发区面积为23.5×10⁴ km²。

1.6 长江经济带岩溶塌陷分布及危险性评价分区图
The Distribution Map of Karst Collapses and Hazard Assessment in the Yangtze River Economic Zone

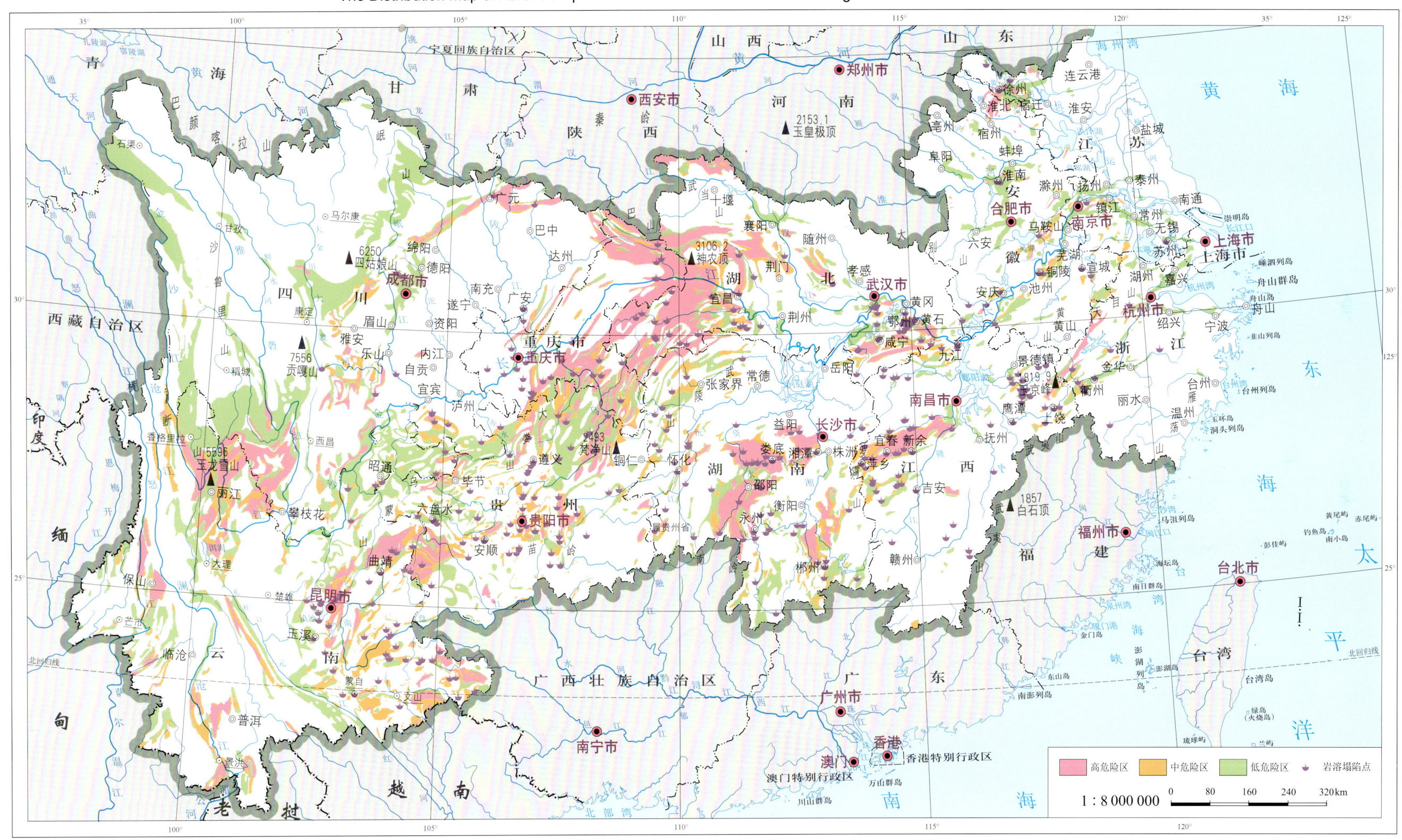

岩溶塌陷分布：全区有岩溶塌陷805处，仅有1处为基岩塌陷，其他均为土层塌陷。除上海外，各省市均有发育，其中，以云南、贵州、湖南、安徽和江西最为发育。在805处岩溶塌陷中，按成因统计有608处为人类工程活动所诱发，154处为自然条件下产生。以矿山疏干排水、地下水开采、交通工程施工为代表的人类工程活动是岩溶塌陷的主要诱发因素。岩溶塌陷危险性分布：高危险区面积约$23.5×10^4 km^2$，中危险区面积约$11.1×10^4 km^2$，主要分布在贵州、云南、湖北、湖南和重庆。

1.7 长江经济带活动断裂与区域地壳稳定性评价图
The Map of Active Fault Zones and Assessment on Regional Crustal Stability in the Yangtze River Economic Zone

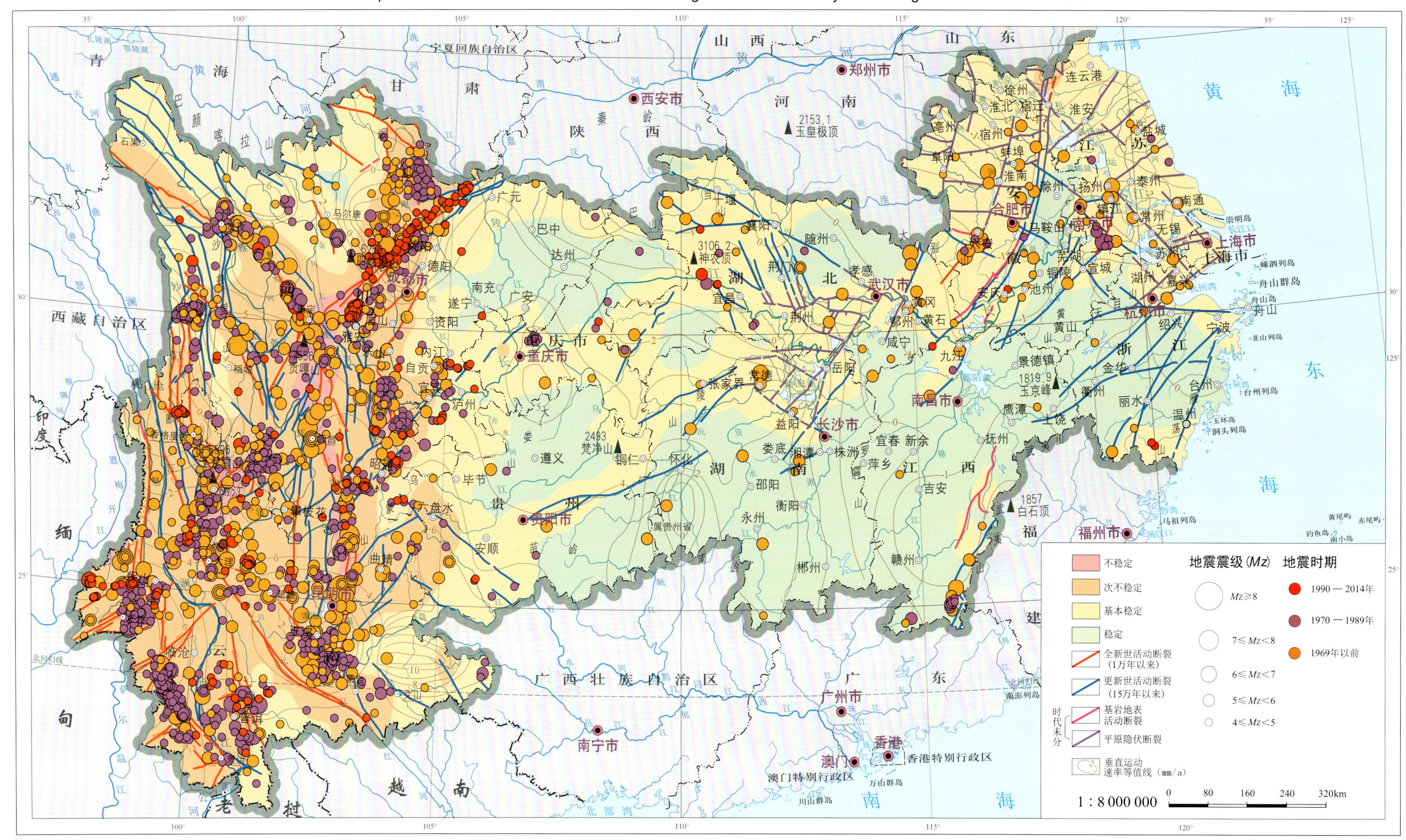

活动断裂分布：15万年以来的活动断裂主要有东门沟断裂带、虎牙断裂、邓柯-甘孜断裂、甘孜-炉霍断裂、茂汶-天全断裂、龙门山断裂带、巴塘断裂、剑川-三江口断裂、丽江-宁蒗断裂、安宁河断裂、麻城-团风断裂、茅山断裂、瑞金-会昌断裂、郯庐断裂带等。区域地壳稳定性分区特征：稳定区占32.6%，基本稳定区占36.6%，次不稳定区占28.2%，不稳定区占2.6%。稳定区和基本稳定区主要分布在长江经济带中东部；不稳定区主要分布在眉山市—金阳县—昆明市一带和丽江市—剑川县一带、甘洛县—盐津县一带地区。

1.8 长三角经济区地面沉降与地裂缝现状图
The Situation Map of Ground Subsidence and Ground Fissures in the Yangtze River Economic Zone

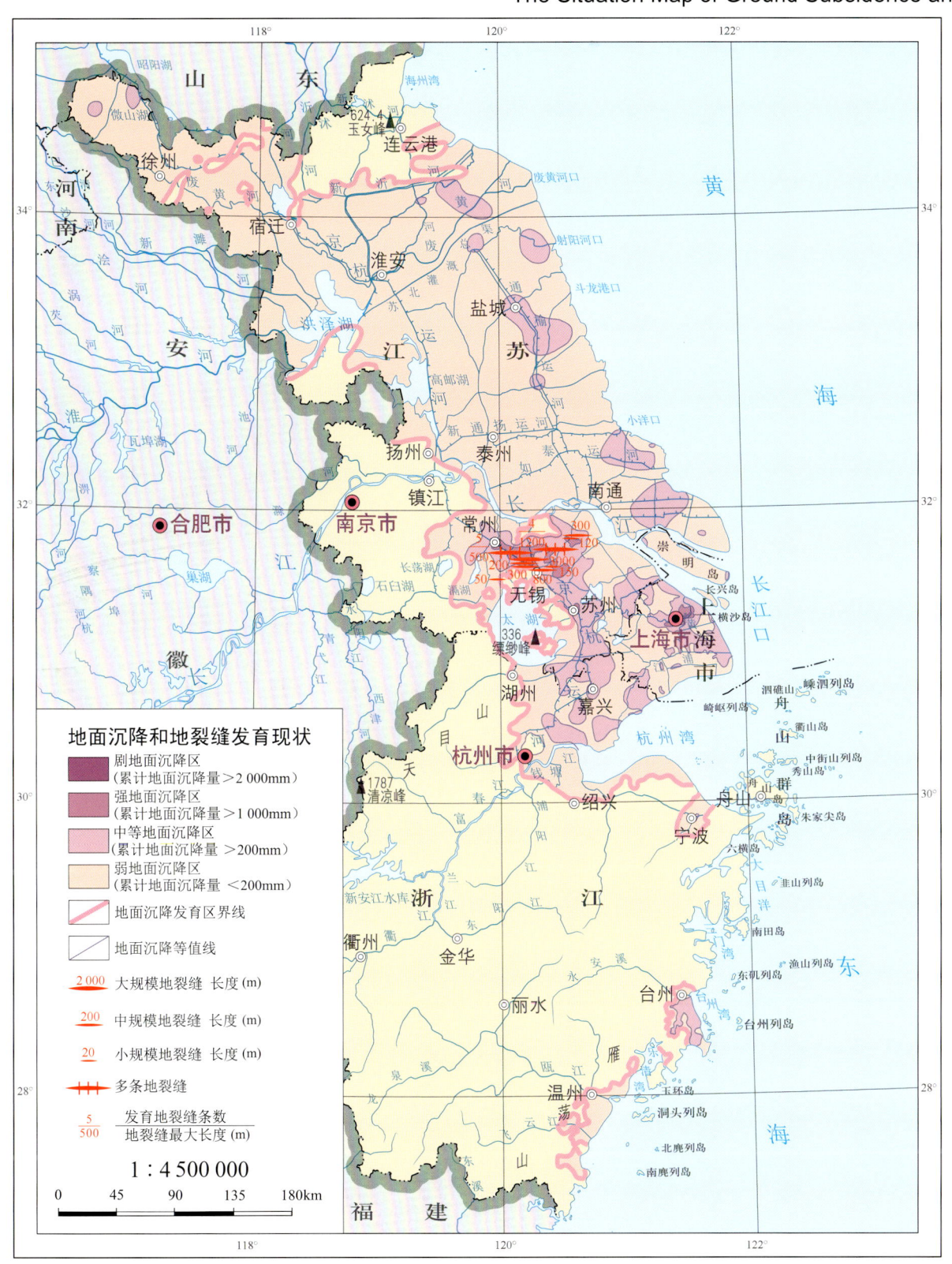

地面沉降使得上海外滩防汛墙4次被加高

地面沉降导致上海一些桥洞净空减少、江河运力下降

无锡锡山区锡北镇杨墅里地裂缝及引起的房屋开裂现象

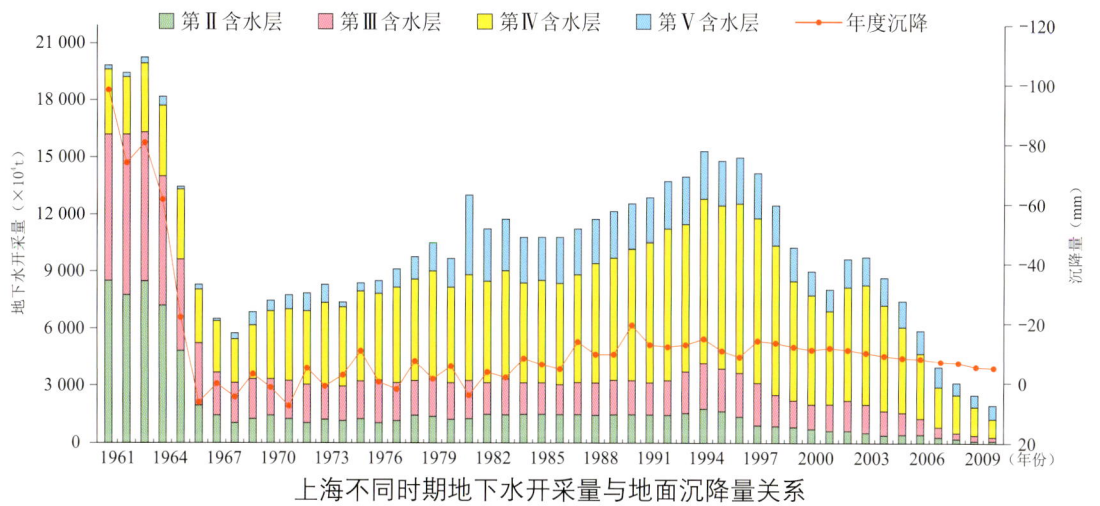

上海不同时期地下水开采量与地面沉降量关系

江苏省苏锡常、浙江省杭嘉湖及上海市累积沉降量超200mm范围已达1/3，面积超过10 000km²，在区域上有连片的趋势；江苏盐城、连云港等沿海平原区累积地面沉降量超过200mm的区域面积为9 300km²。长三角经济区地面沉降造成直接和间接损失约3 629.1亿元。

产业发展规划布局需要考虑的能源与资源潜力

Energy and Resources Potentiality Needing Consideration for Planning and Layout of Industrial Development

2

2.1 长江经济带能源矿产资源分布图
The Distribution Map of Energy Mineral Resources in the Yangtze River Economic Zone

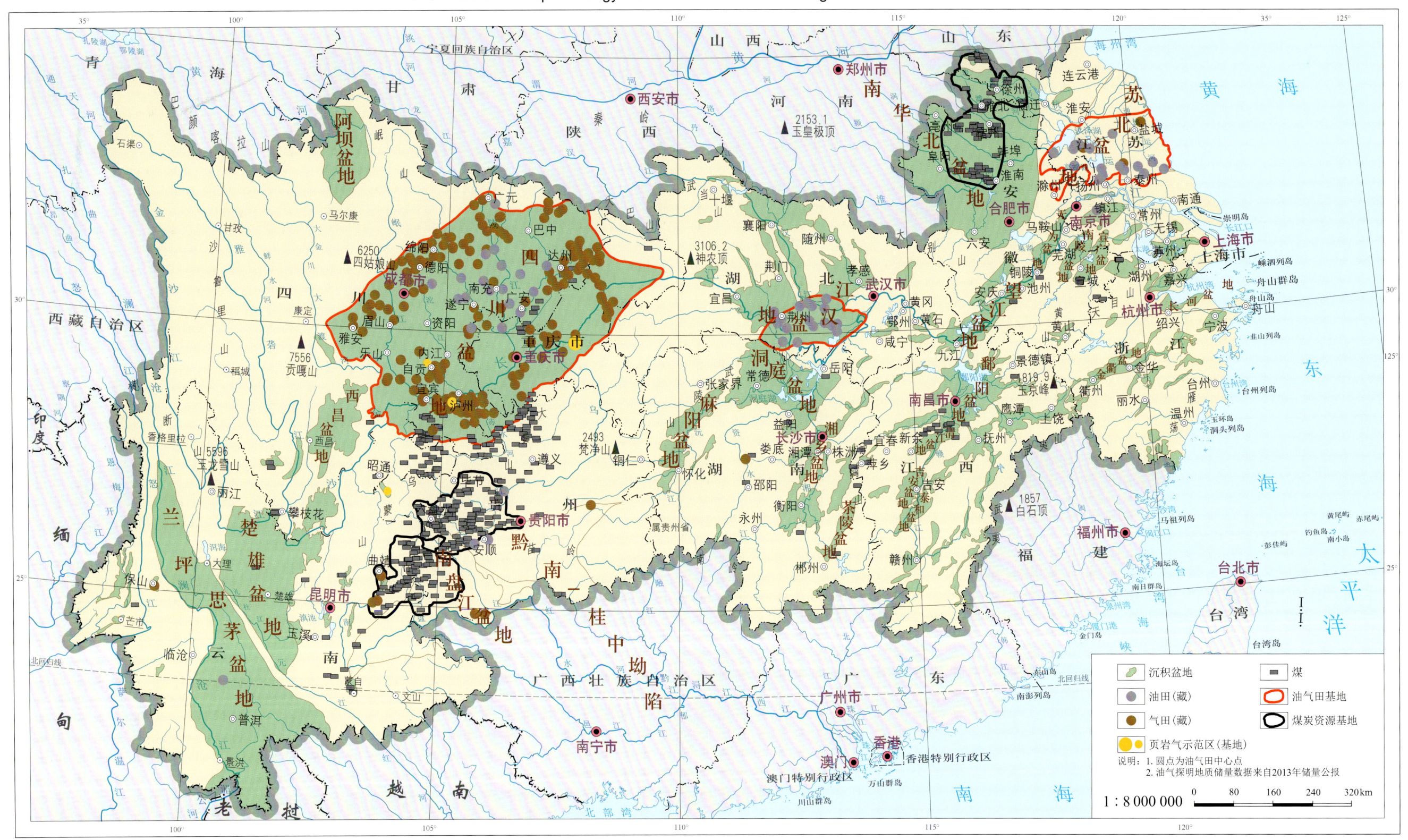

能源矿产主要为石油、天然气、页岩气和煤等。油气田主要分布于四川盆地、江汉盆地和苏北盆地，共发现油田93个，气田97个；页岩气勘探在四川涪陵获得突破。至2013年底，探明可采石油储量1.41×10^{8}t，探明天然气储量18 719.87m^3，累计石油产量8.6×10^{8}t、天然气产量4 292.94×10^{8}m^3。至2014年底，累计探明页岩气地质储量1067.5×10^{8}m^3，累计产量15×10^{8}m^3。至2012年底，探明煤炭矿产地432处（超大型28处，大型141处），有近50%的矿产地处于开采状态。至2014年11月，累计探获煤炭资源储量1463.09×10^{8}t，保有储量1037×10^{8}t。

2.2 长江经济带地热资源分布图
The Distribution Map of Geothermal Resources in the Yangtze River Economic Zone

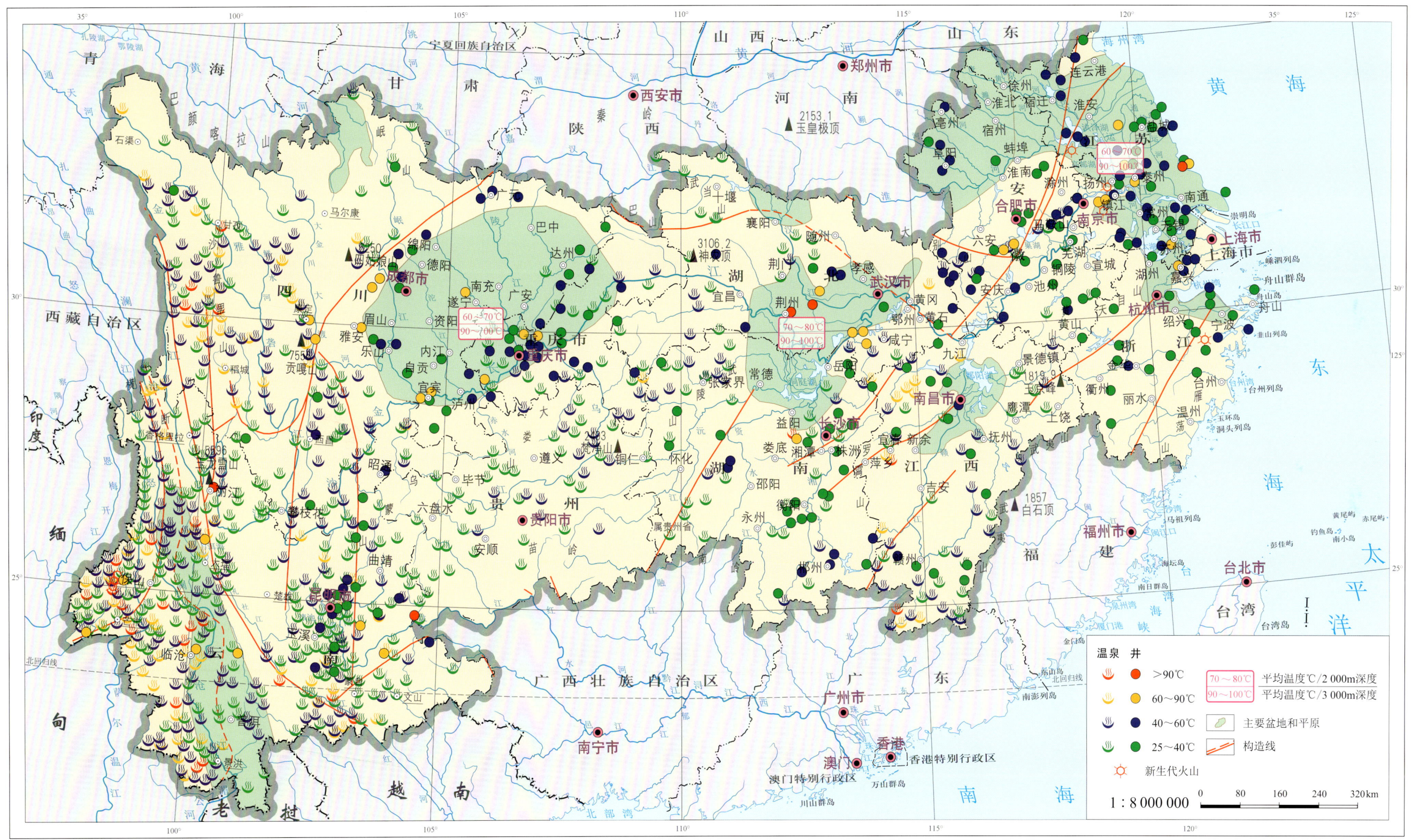

长江经济带地热资源分布特征：区内沉积盆地传导型热储主要分布在苏北盆地、江汉盆地和四川盆地等；隆起山地断裂型热储主要分布在滇西隆滑高原、断隆山地高中温热储区；对流型热储主要分布在川西滇东和东南沿海等。1 000m深度地温平均为40~45℃，2 000m深度地温平均为60~80℃，3 000m深度地温平均为90~110℃。长江经济带地热资源开发潜力大，区内地下热水可采资源量估算为16.090 37×10⁸m³/a。

2.3 长江经济带矿产资源开发利用图
The Exploitation Map of Mineral Resources in the Yangtze River Economic Zone

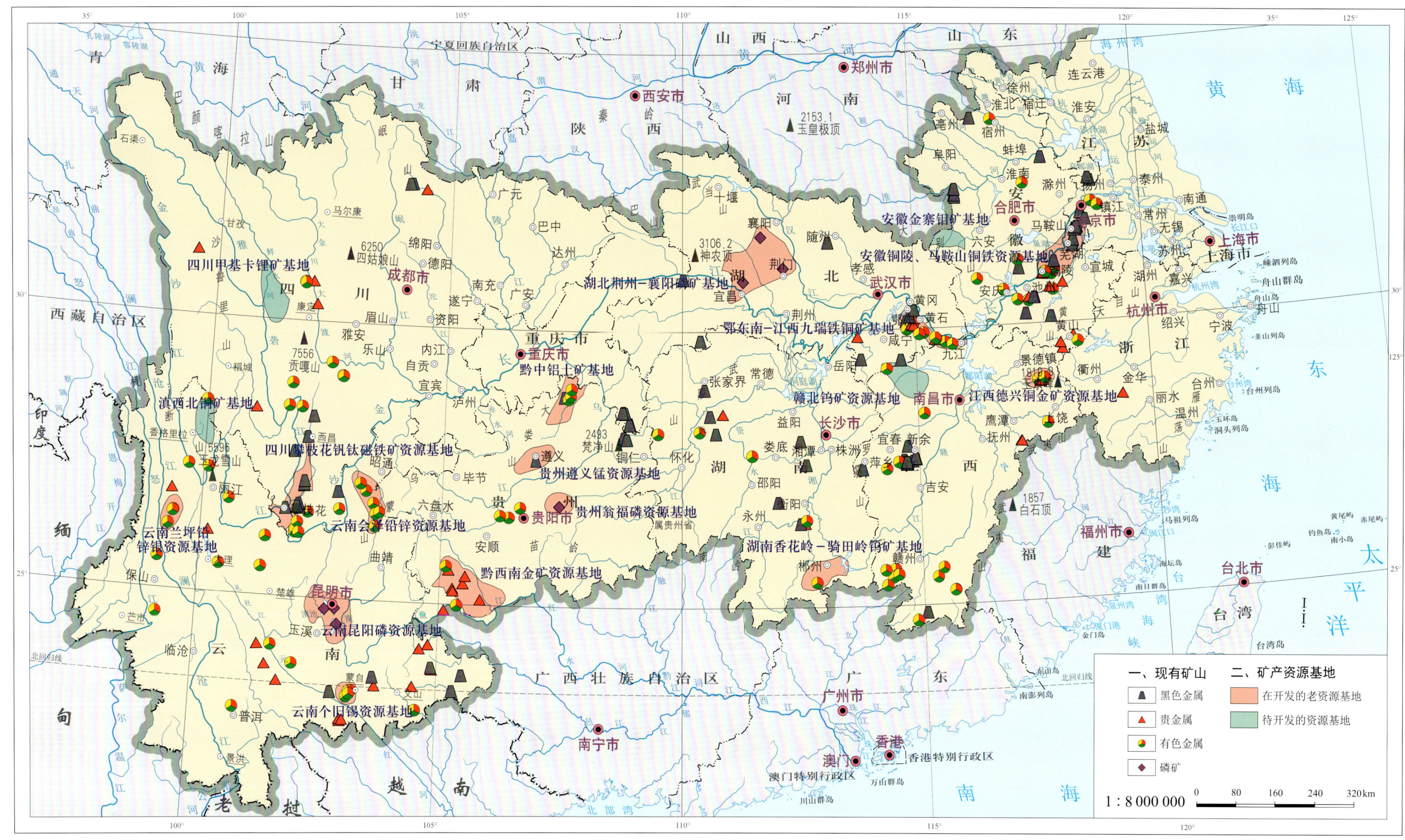

矿产资源开发利用程度较高，是国家重要资源供给的核心区域，但规模化、集约化水平总体不高。现有矿山48 000万个，在许多地区已成为重要大型资源产业基地，包括江西德兴铜金矿资源基地、赣南钨矿资源基地、四川攀枝花钒钛磁铁矿资源基地、黔西南金矿资源基地、贵州遵义锰资源基地、云南昆阳磷资源基地、云南兰坪铅锌银资源基地、云南会泽铅锌资源基地、云南个旧锡资源基地等。2013年，矿业工业总产值为4 960.8亿元，从业人员超过300万人，发展起来的资源型城市99座。但传统的资源开发利用方式也带来了生态环境问题，迫切需要绿色转型。

2.4 长江经济带矿产资源潜力图
The Distribution Map of Mineral Resources Potentiality in the Yangtze River Economic Zone

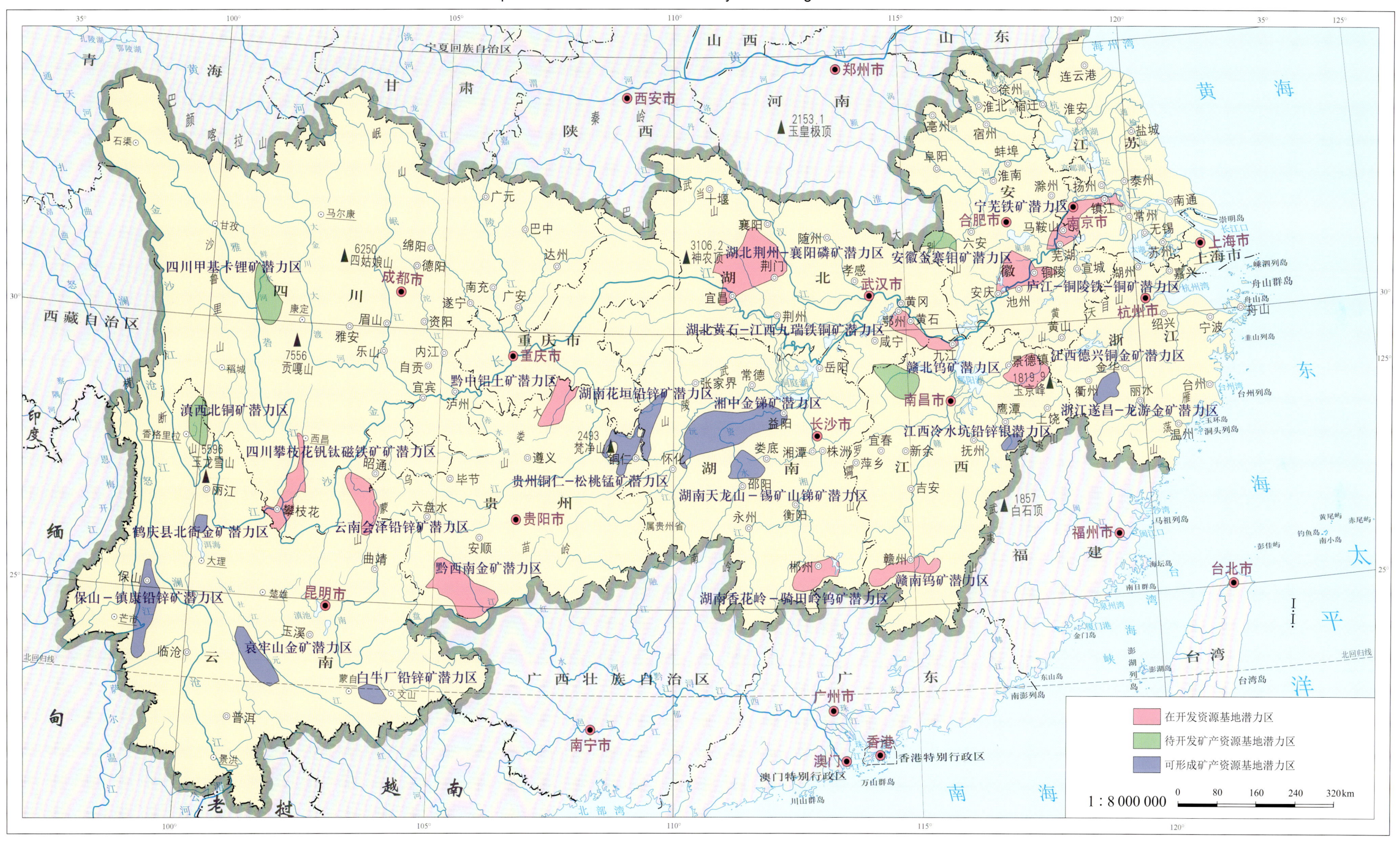

长江经济带矿产资源具有良好的开采潜力，现已形成7处矿产潜力区，分布于江苏南京、安徽芜湖和铜陵、江西德兴和九江、湖北荆州—襄阳、四川攀枝花、贵州安顺、云南会泽等地，面积约1.46×10⁴km²，矿种类型为铁、铜、铅、锌、金、磷、铝土矿等。新形成矿产资源潜力区有4处，分布于安徽金寨、江西南昌、四川雅安、云南丽江等地，面积约0.34×10⁴km²，矿种类型为铜、钨、钼、锂等。目前尚存在9处可开发利用潜力区，主要分布于江西芜州、浙江遂昌—龙游、湖南西部、云南西南部，面积约0.96×10⁴km²，矿种类型为铅、锌、金、锑、锡等。

2.5 长江经济带金属矿产资源分布图
The Distribution Map of Metal Mineral Resources in the Yangtze River Economic Zone

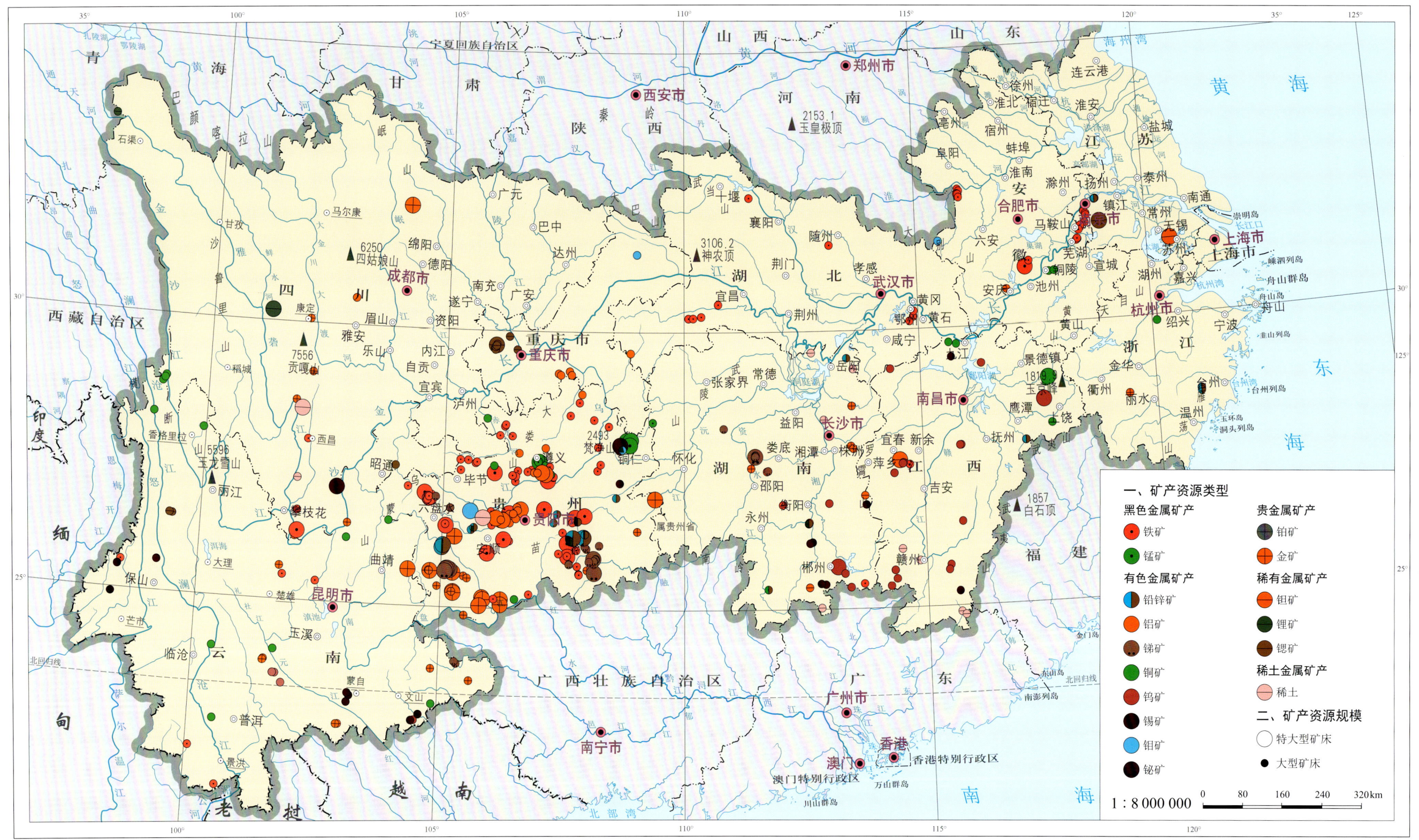

金属矿产资源丰富，保有储量占全国50%以上的矿种有30种，钨、锑、离子型稀土等在世界占据优势。至2012年底，探明中型及其以上矿产地1 439处（超大型93处）；黑色金属矿产中探明大型—超大型铁矿石量105.42×10⁸t、锰矿石资源量23 713.4×10⁴t。至2013年底，有色金属矿产探明大型—超大型铜金属量3 366.45×10⁴t、铝土矿4.14×10⁸t、铅锌6 733.6×10⁴t。氧化钨560.5×10⁴t、锡436.8×10⁴t；贵金属矿产累计探明大型—超大型金2 355.36t、铂73.3t、银（含伴生）6.21×10⁴t。

2.6 长江经济带非金属矿产资源分布图
The Distribution Map of Nonmetallic Minerals Resources in the Yangtze River Economic Zone

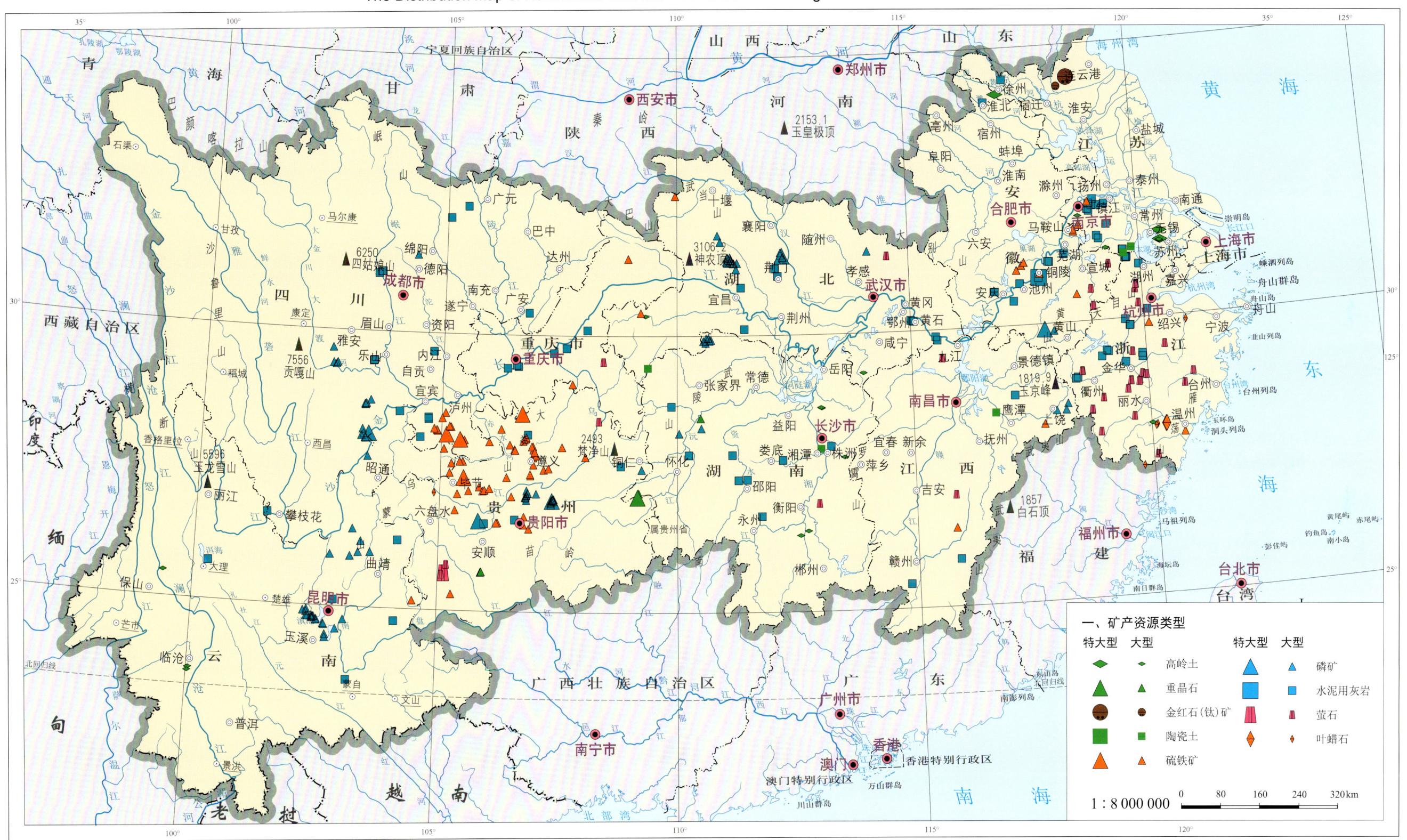

非金属矿产资源丰富，种类繁多。磷矿种的保有储量占全国的89%~90%。我国在世界上占据优势的萤石、重晶石等矿产均集中于本区。至2013年底，累计探明大型—超大型磷矿石123.32×10⁸t，萤石4 050.5×10⁴t。按用途可分为特种非金属矿产，农用肥原料，化工原料，玻璃、陶瓷、耐火材料原料，水泥、砖瓦原料，冶金熔剂及铸型材料等。已探明中—超大型规模非金属矿产地达2 104处，其中大型—超大型矿产地为786处。萤石、磷矿、硫铁矿、玻璃、陶瓷及水泥用等原材料资源占据优势，且大于60%的非金属矿产已处于开采状态。

2.7 长江经济带地下水资源分布图
The Distribution Map of Groundwater Resources in the Yangtze River Economic Zone

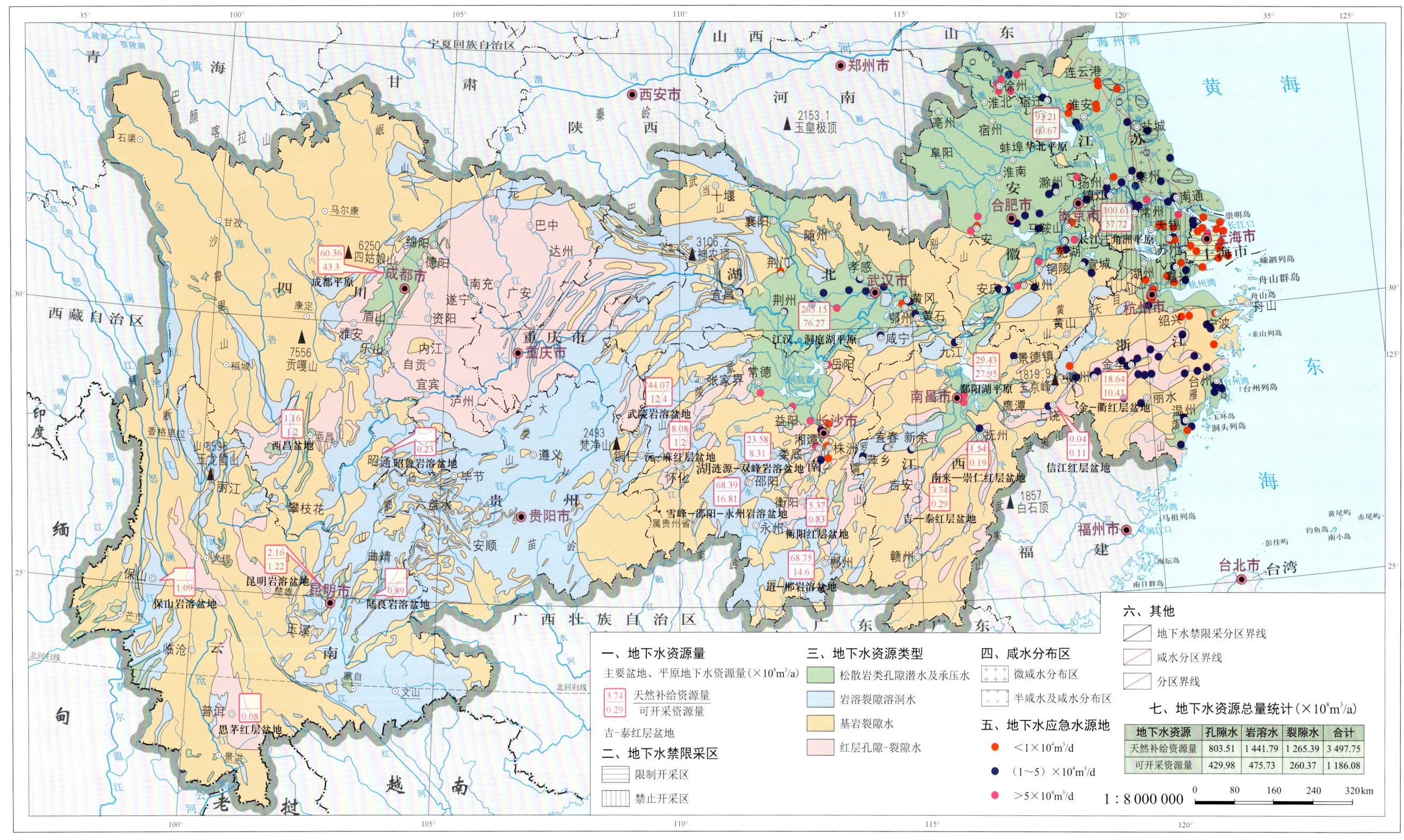

长江经济带地下水资源总量为 $3497.75×10^8m^3/a$，占全国地下水资源总量的37.8%。地下水资源中淡水资源量 $3388.97×10^8m^3/a$，占96.89%，分布于内陆地区。至2002年，地下水可采资源量 $1186.08×10^8m^3/a$，占总量的33.9%。其中，孔隙水可采资源量 $429.98×10^8m^3/a$。地下水禁限开采：长三角地区由于过量开采深层地下水产生地面沉降和地裂缝，对地下水实施禁限采是控制地面沉降的有效措施，苏锡常及杭嘉湖地区为禁采区，上海、南通、盐城和台州等地区为限采区。

3 耕地保护和管理需要重视的土地质量地球化学背景

Land Quality and Geochemical Background Needing Concern in the Protection and Management for Cultivated Land

3.1 长江经济带平原丘陵区绿色农产品产地适宜性分区图

The Suitability Zoning Map for the Plantation of Green Agricultural Products in Plain and Hilly Areas in the Yangtze River Economic Zone

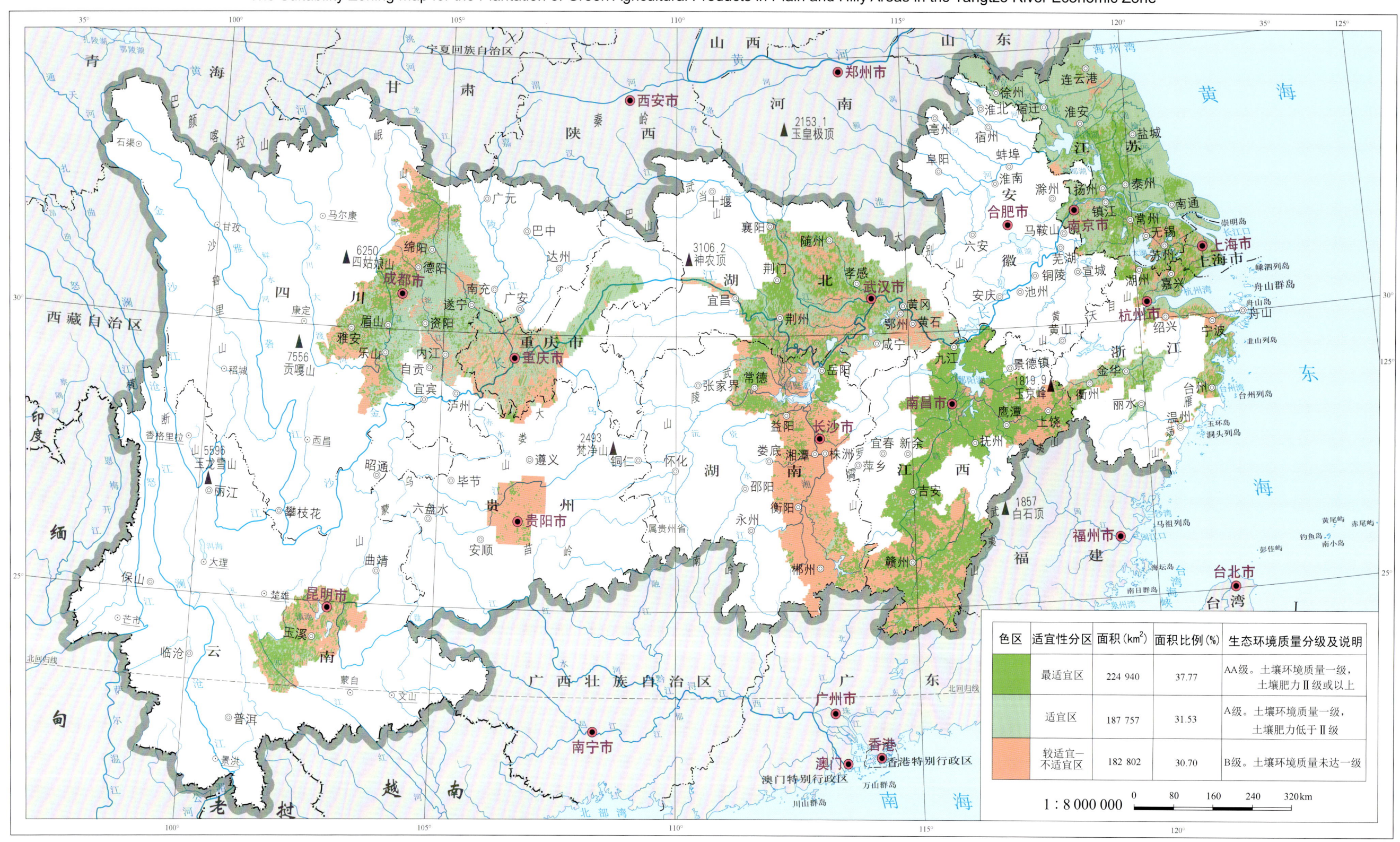

色区	适宜性分区	面积(km²)	面积比例(%)	生态环境质量分级及说明
	最适宜区	224 940	37.77	AA级。土壤环境质量一级，土壤肥力Ⅱ级或以上
	适宜区	187 757	31.53	A级。土壤环境质量一级，土壤肥力低于Ⅱ级
	较适宜—不适宜区	182 802	30.70	B级。土壤环境质量未达一级

1:8 000 000

根据已完成的长江经济带上海、江苏等9省2市1:25万多目标区域地球化学调查获得的表层土壤54种元素和指标高精度定量分析数据，以及对应的地貌、土壤和土地利用类型数据，区内平原土壤绿色农产品种植最适宜区—适宜区面积为41.27×10⁴km²，占评价区的69.30%，主要分布于环太湖、里下河平原、江淮、环鄱阳湖、江汉平原、成都平原和云南玉溪；较适宜—不适宜区为18.28×10⁴km²，占30.70%，大面积分布于湖南和贵州，斑块状分布于黄石、仙桃、贵阳、昆明、成都盆地山前地带，以及赣南、赣东北、铜陵、宁绍平原、杭嘉湖平原、滁州、宿州和连云港等地。

3.2 长江经济带平原丘陵区土地有益元素综合分区图
The Integrated Zoning Map of Beneficial Elements in Soil in Plain and Hilly Areas in the Yangtze River Economic Zone

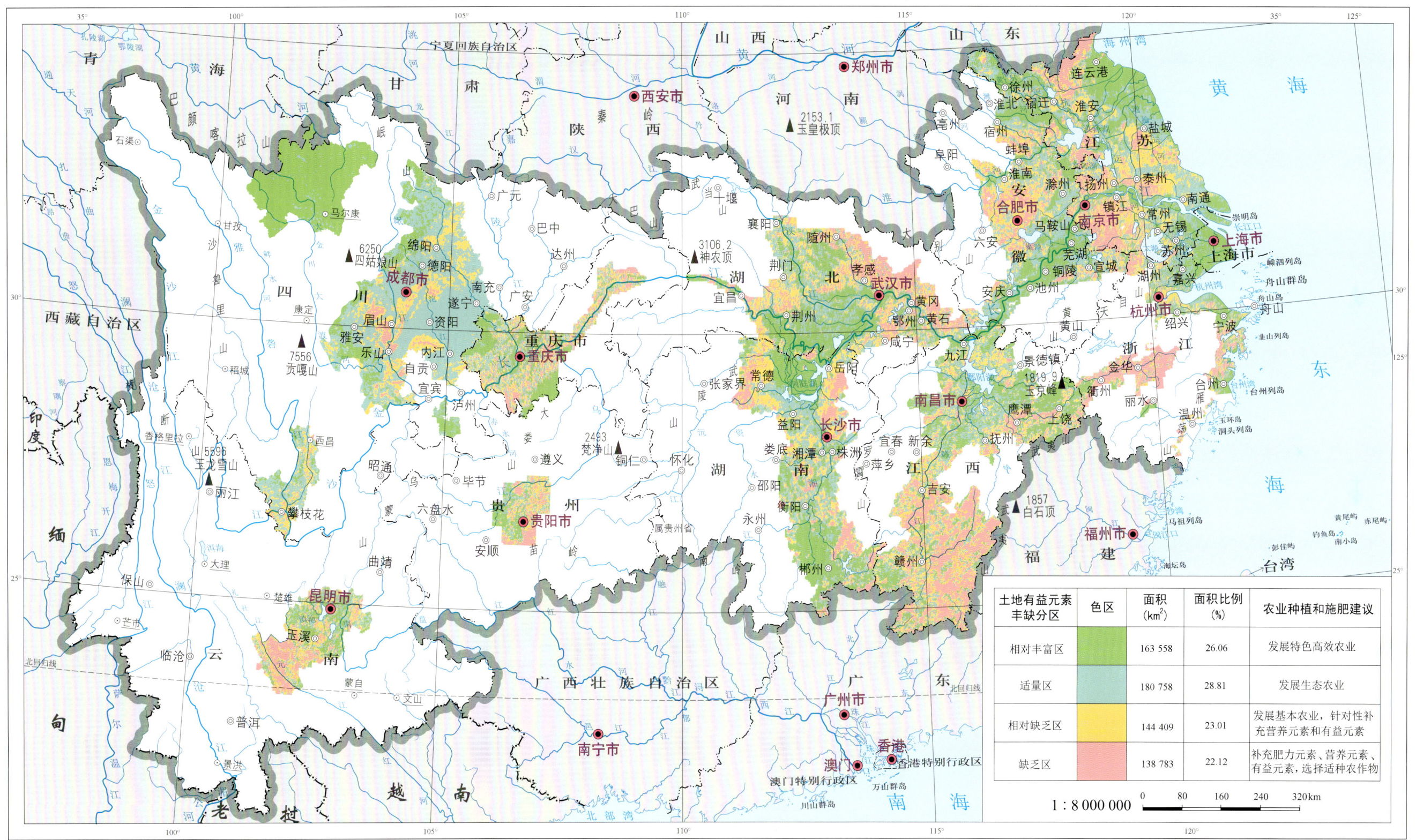

土地有益元素丰缺分区	色区	面积 (km²)	面积比例 (%)	农业种植和施肥建议
相对丰富区		163 558	26.06	发展特色高效农业
适量区		180 758	28.81	发展生态农业
相对缺乏区		144 409	23.01	发展基本农业，针对性补充营养元素和有益元素
缺乏区		138 783	22.12	补充肥力元素、营养元素、有益元素，选择适种农作物

1:8 000 000

根据已完成的长江经济带上海、江苏等9省2市1:25万多目标区域地球化学调查获得的表层土壤N、C、P、K、S、Ca、Mg、Cl、B、Fe、Si、Mn、Mo、V、Zn、Cu、Co、I、F、Se和pH值共21项指标高精度定量分析数据，以及对应的地貌类型、土壤类型和土地利用类型数据，区内土地有益元素适量以上面积为$34.43×10^4 km^2$，占54.87%，大部分面积分布于四川阿坝、成都盆地、环洞庭湖、环鄱阳湖、安徽沿江、苏北沿海和杭嘉湖平原；较缺乏区面积为$13.88×10^4 km^2$，占22.12%，分布于赣南、江淮、鄂东北以及云南玉溪等地。

长江经济带国土资源与重大地质问题图集
TATLAS OF LAND RESOURCES AND MOMENTOUS GEOLOGICAL PROBLEMS IN YANGTZE RIVER ECONOMIC ZONE

3.3 长江经济带土壤类型图
The Map of Soil Types in the Yangtze River Economic Zone

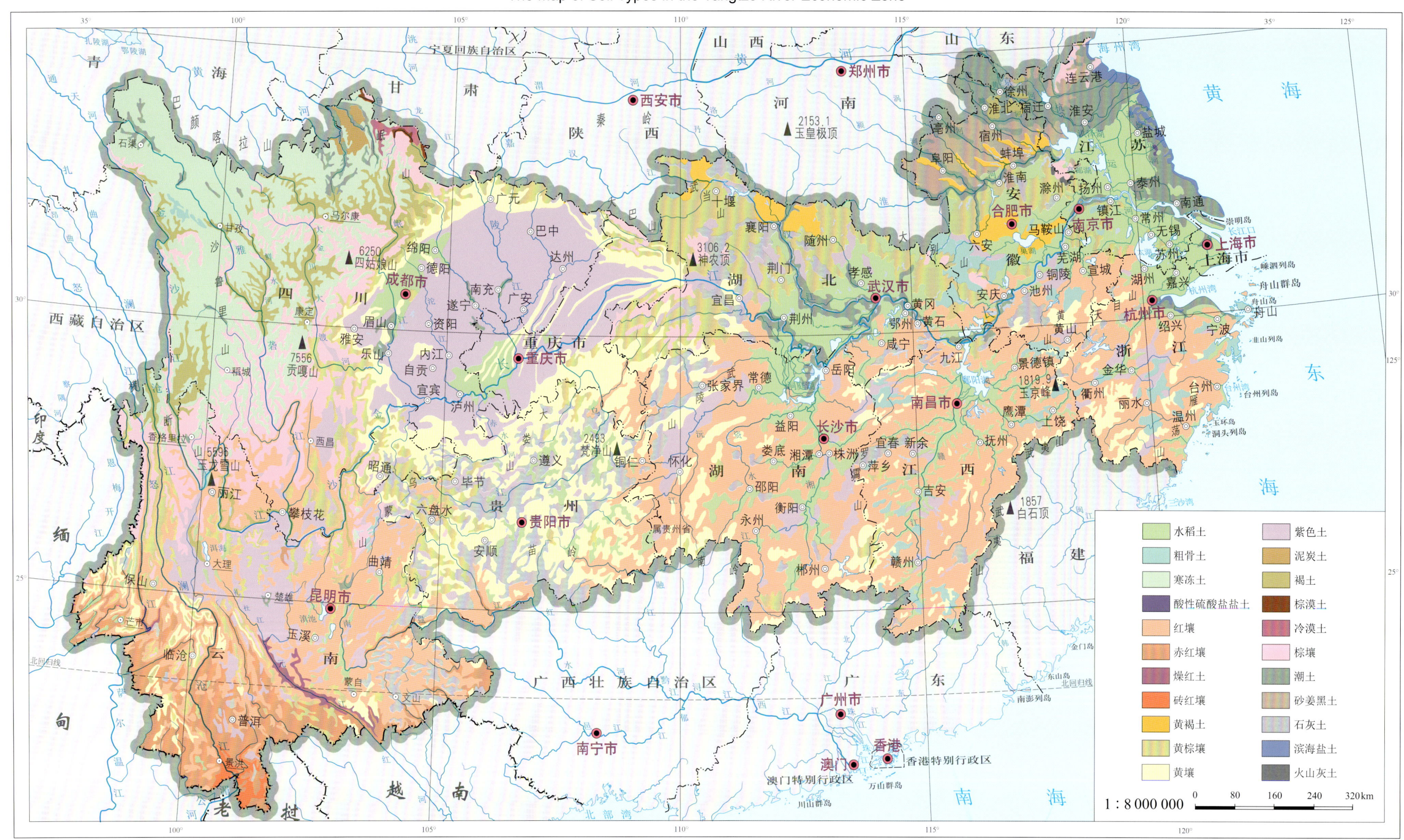

长江经济带土壤按土类划分为水稻土、红壤、紫色土、黄壤、潮土、粗骨土、石灰土、黄棕壤、滨海盐土、砖红壤、赤红壤、燥红壤、砂姜黑土、火山灰土、黄褐土、褐土、冷漠土、棕壤、棕漠土、寒冻土、泥炭土、酸性硫酸盐盐土共22种。分布最广的土壤类型为水稻土、红壤、紫色土、黄壤等。水稻土主要分布于成都平原、长江中下游平原、滨海平原，山间谷地及缓坡地段也有分布；红壤主要分布于长江南岸的丘陵山区；紫色土主要分布于四川、重庆、云南地区的丘陵阶地上；黄壤主要分布于贵州、四川、江西、浙江等省山区。

3.4 长江经济带耕地分布图
The Distribution Map of Cultivated Land in the Yangtze River Economic Zone

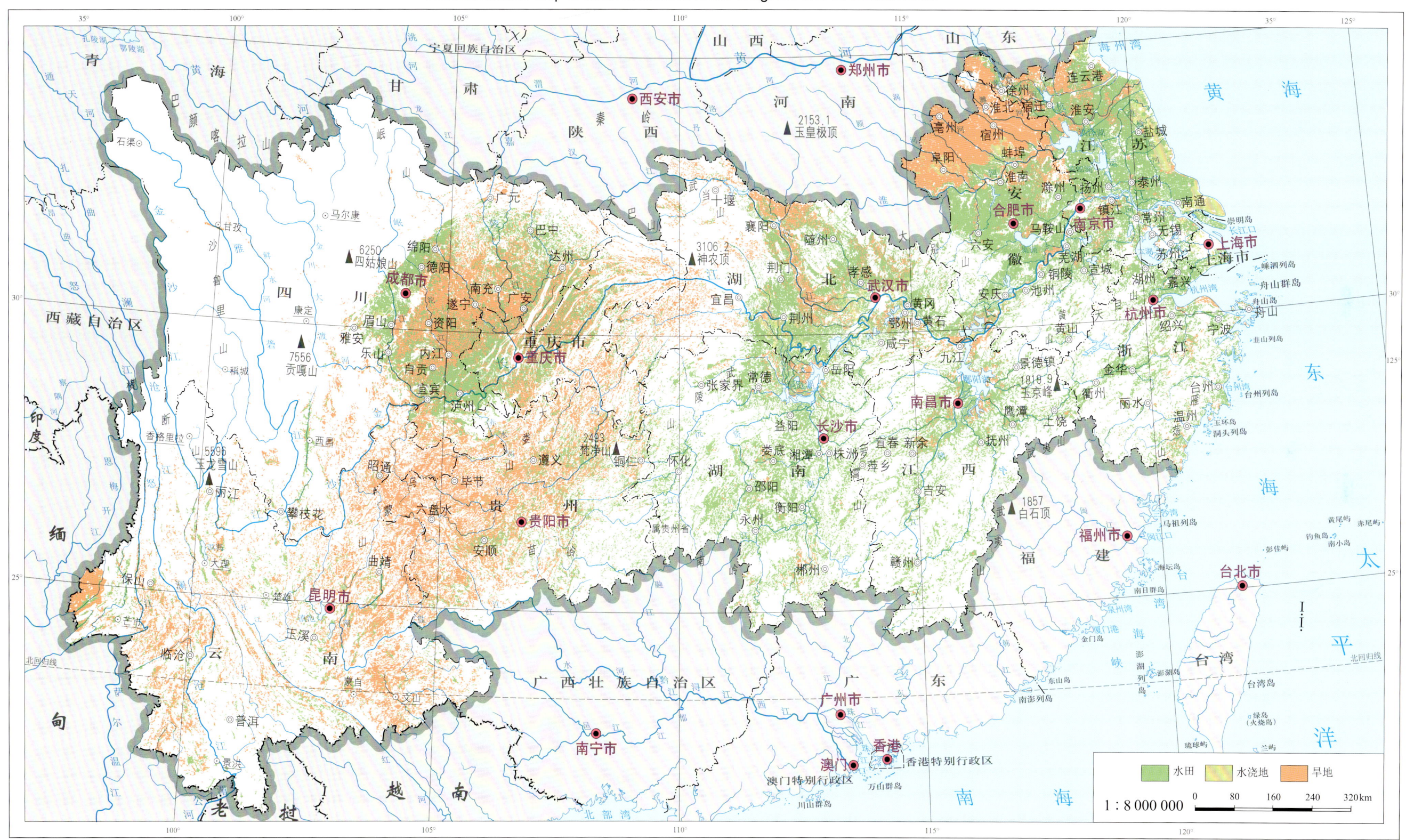

长江经济带耕地类型主要分水田、水浇地和旱地3类。第一类是水田，在湖南省、湖北省的中部和东部，安徽省中部、江苏省大部地区均有集中分布，浙江省、江西省也以水田为主，在云、贵、川三省也有水田的零散分布，是长江经济带最主要的耕地类型；第二类是旱地，主要位于四川盆地中部，湖北省、安徽省、江苏省北部，在云南、贵州两省也有零散的分布；第三类是水浇地，主要位于江苏省东部的沿海地区，其他地区也有零散分布，此种地类所占面积相对较少。

3.5 长江经济带平原丘陵区土地环境质量综合分区图
The Integrated Zoning Map of Land and Environmental Quality in Plain and Hilly Areas in the Yangtze River Economic Zone

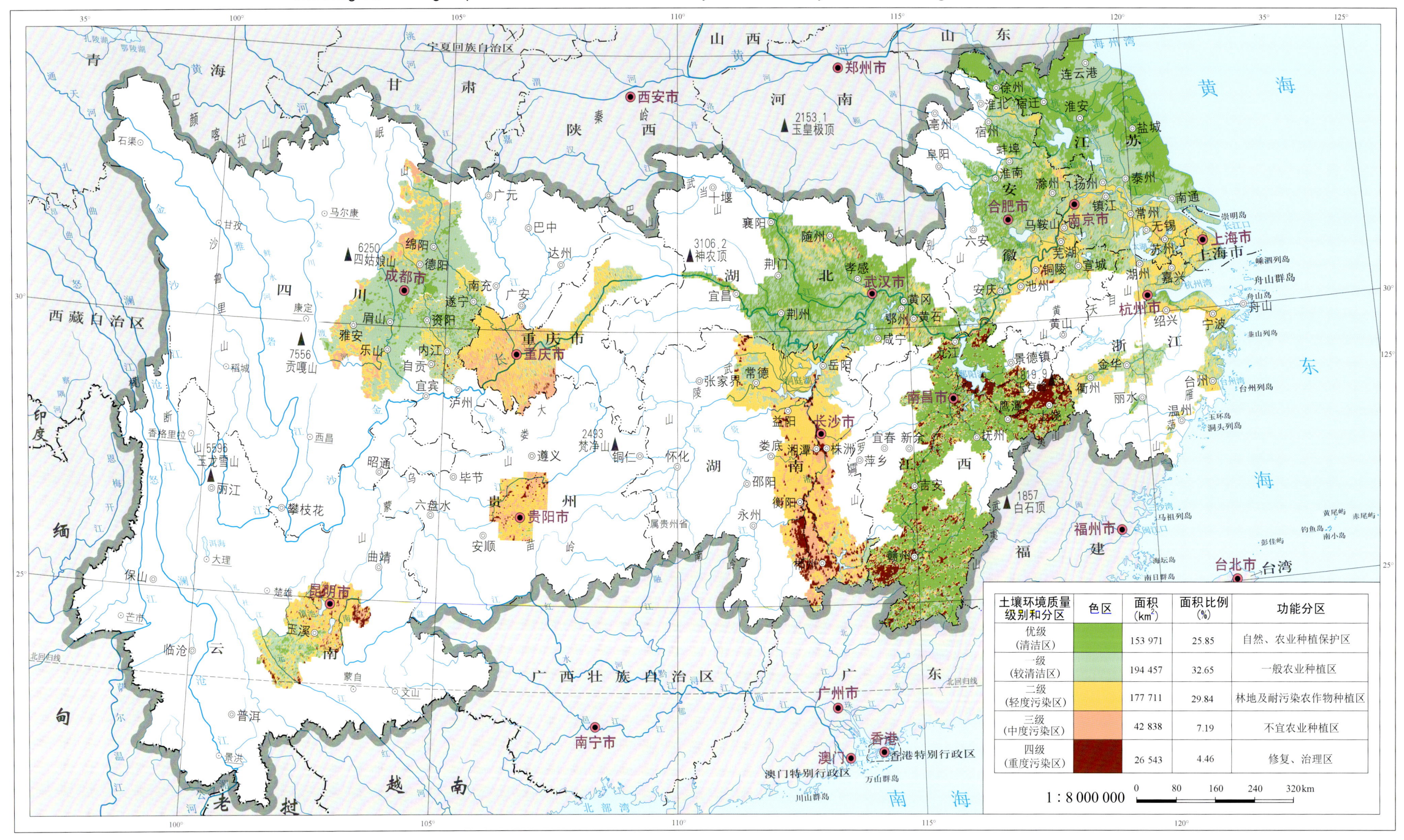

根据已完成的长江经济带上海、江苏等9省2市1:25万多目标区域地球化学调查获得的表层土壤54种元素和指标高精度定量分析数据，以及对应的地貌、土壤和土地利用类型数据，长江经济带平原土壤环境质量总体良好，一级以上土壤面积为$34.84×10^4km^2$，占评价区的58.51%。其中优级土壤面积为$15.40×10^4km^2$，大面积分布于苏北、江淮、江汉平原和成都平原等地区，三级以下土壤面积为$6.94×10^4km^2$，呈斑块及星点状分布于赣东北、赣南、湖南长沙—郴州等地。

3.6 长三角经济区平原土地质量地球化学分区图
The Geochemical Zoning Map for Land Quality in the Plain in the Yangtze River Delta Economic Zone

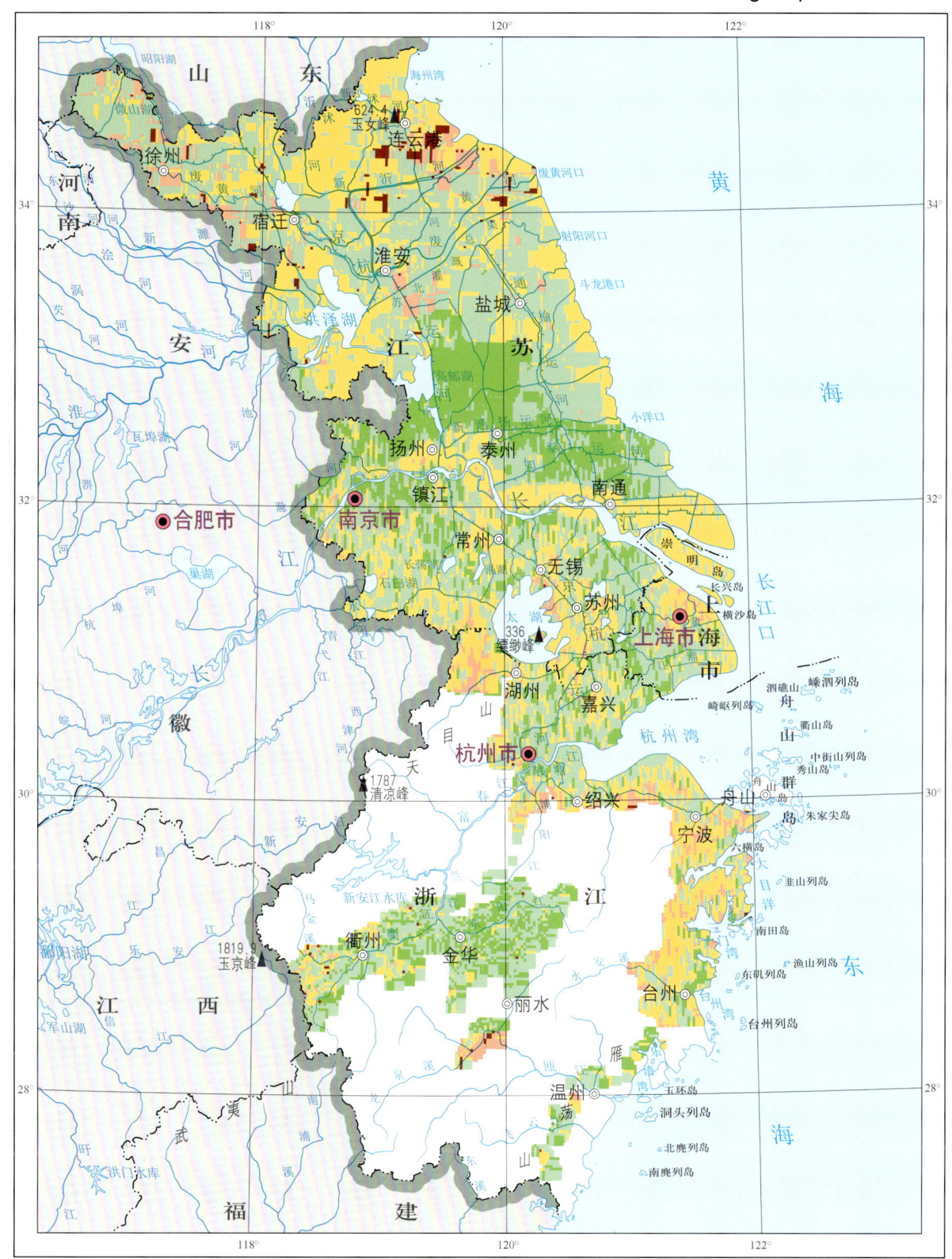

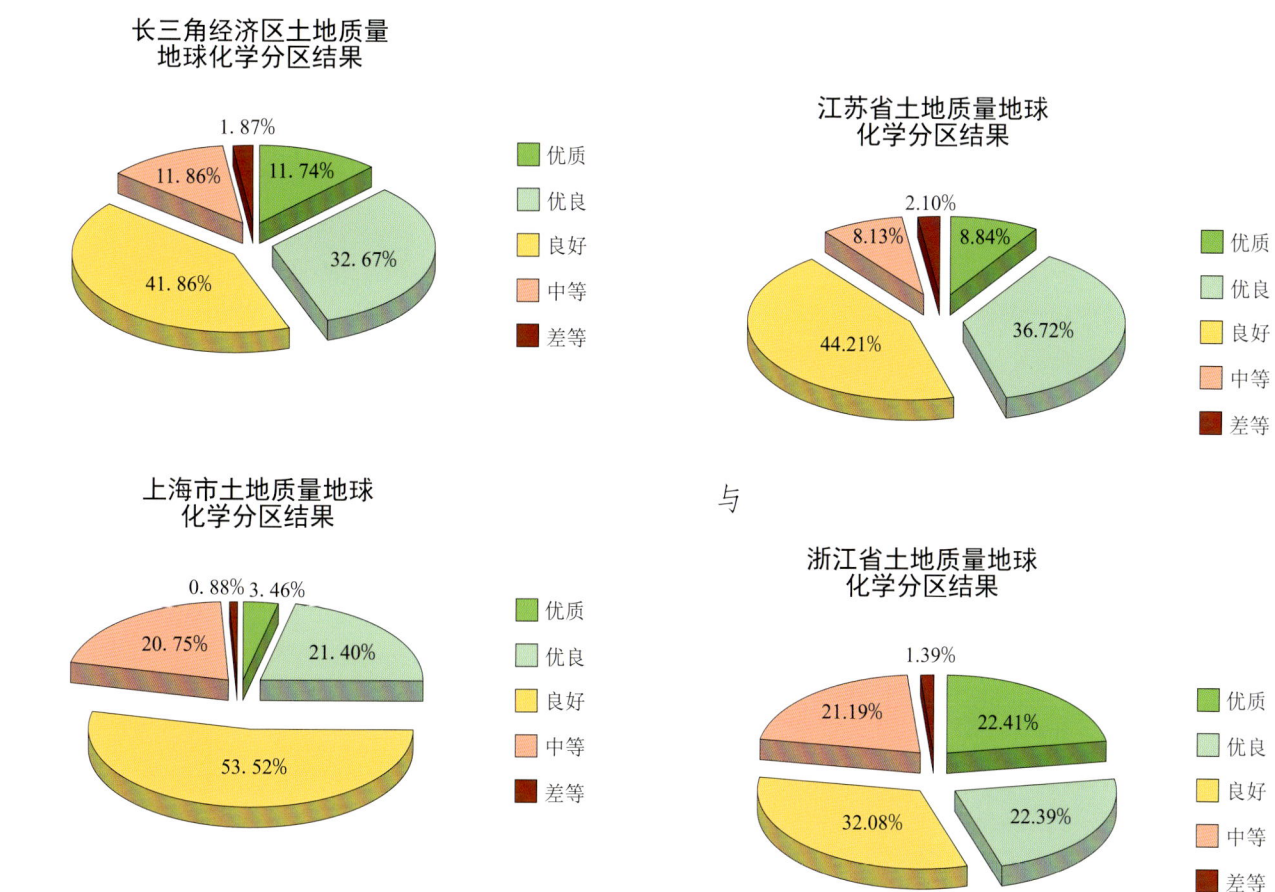

长三角经济区平原土地质量整体尚可，良好以上等级土壤为 $11.71×10^4 km^2$，占评价区的86.27%。优质级土壤为 $1.59×10^4 km^2$，占11.74%，主要分布于里下河地区和金华盆地。差等级土壤为 $2 534 km^2$，占1.87%，主要呈星点状分布于区内。

土地质量 地化分区	色区	面积 (km²)	比例 (%)	功能分区
优 质		15 936	11.74	土壤环境清洁、养分丰富 至中等。绿色农业种植区
优 良		44 362	32.67	土壤环境尚清洁、养分 中等。自然、农业保护区
良 好		56 841	41.86	土壤环境轻度污染 一般农业种植区
中 等		16 108	11.86	土壤环境中度污染 林地及耐污染农作物种植区
差 等		2 534	1.87	土壤环境重度污染 不宜农业种植区

1 : 4 500 000

国土开发与生态环境保护需要重视的资源环境状况

Resources and Environment Status Needing Attention for Land Exploitation and Ecological Environment Conservation

4

4.1 长江经济带地貌图
The Geomorphologic Map of the Yangtze River Economic Zone

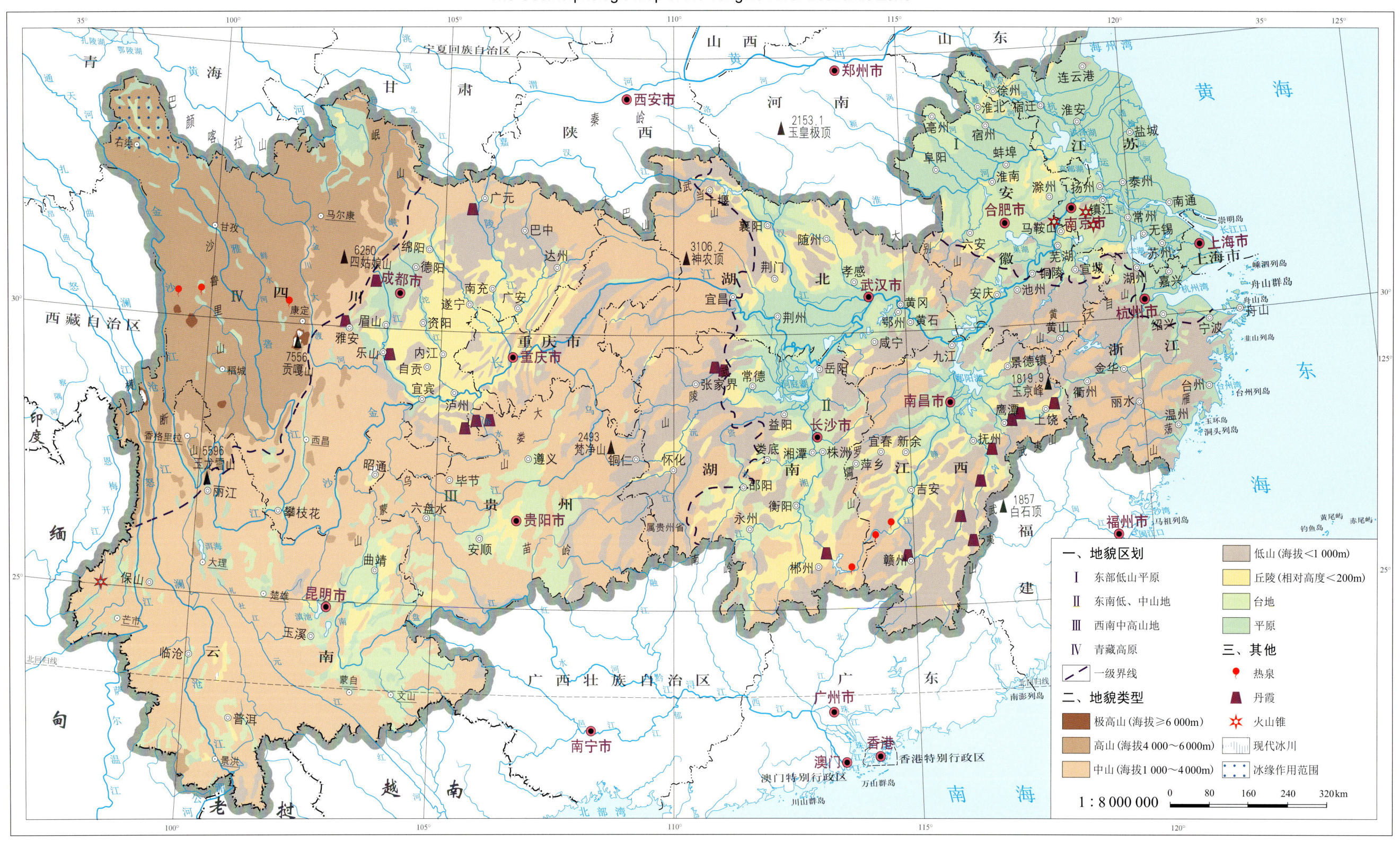

长江经济带地跨我国地势三大阶梯，地貌复杂多样、类型齐全。自西向东大致以广元—丽江、十堰—邵阳、六安—宁波为界划分为4个大区。地貌类型按海拔高度及起伏度划分为7类，分别为极高山、高山、中山、低山、丘陵、台地和平原。大致以十堰—邵阳一线为界，西部主要为山地地貌，东部主要为平原台地地貌；西部大致以广元—丽江一线为界，以西主要为极高山—高山地貌，以东主要为中山地貌；东部地区大致以邵阳—南京一线为界，以南以低山地貌为主，以北以平原为主间夹台地地貌。

4.2 长江经济带国土分类保护区划图
The Zoning Map of Classification for National Lands Protection in the Yangtze River Economic Zone

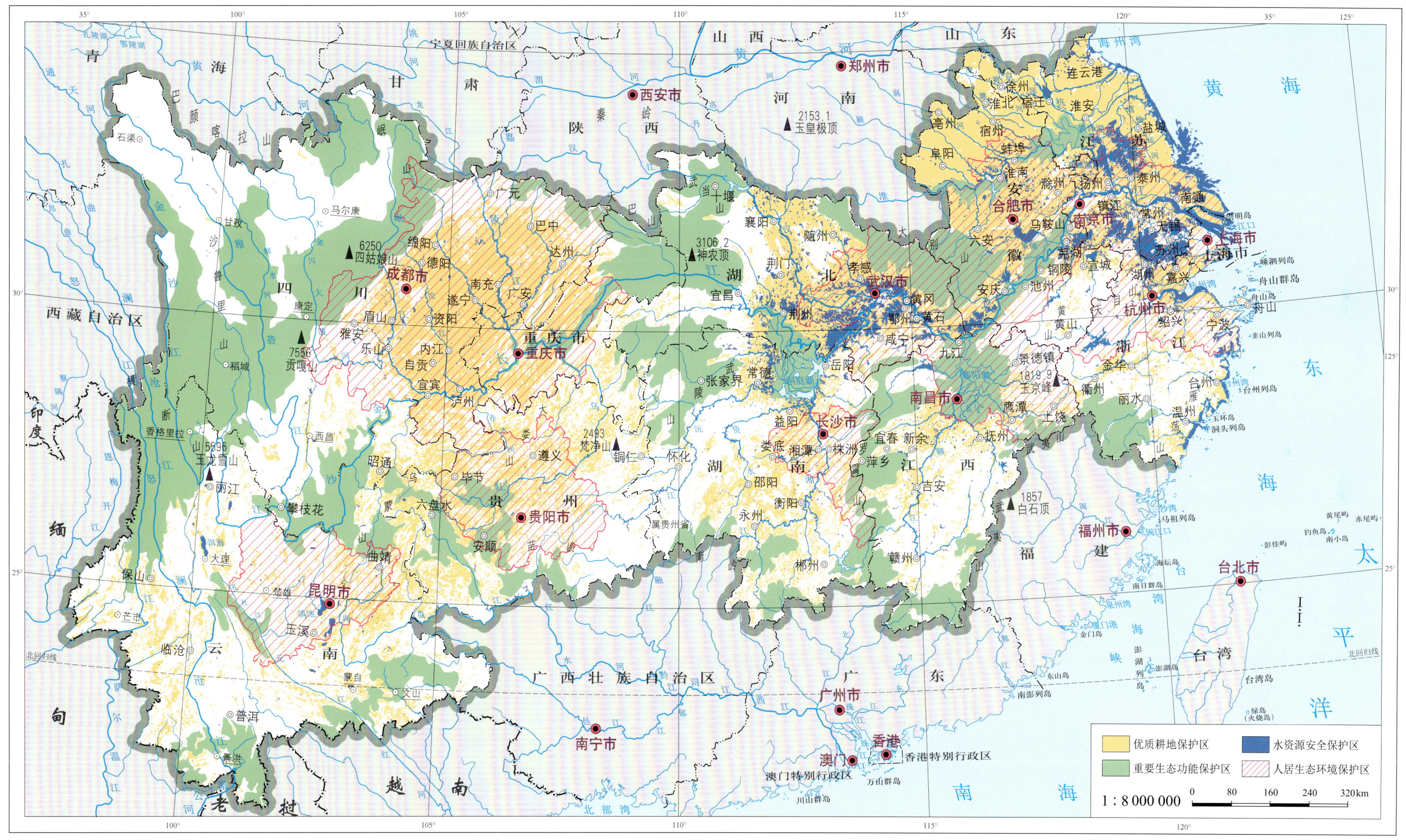

长江经济带主要包含4类保护区域：①优质耕地保护区，指涵盖四川盆地、鄱阳湖平原和洞庭湖平原等地区；②重要生态功能保护区，主要指生物多样性维护功能区、水土保持功能区（如三峡库区）以及鄱阳湖湿地等地区；③水资源安全保护区，主要包括长江干流及其沿岸主要支流和湖泊；④人居生态环境保护区，主要指长三角、江淮、武汉、长株潭、环鄱阳湖、成渝、滇中和黔中城市群。这些地区人口和产业高度集聚，社会经济比较发达，人居生态环境承受较大压力，需要予以重点保护。

4.3 长江经济带生态功能区划图
The Zoning Map of Ecological Function in the Yangtze River Economic Zone

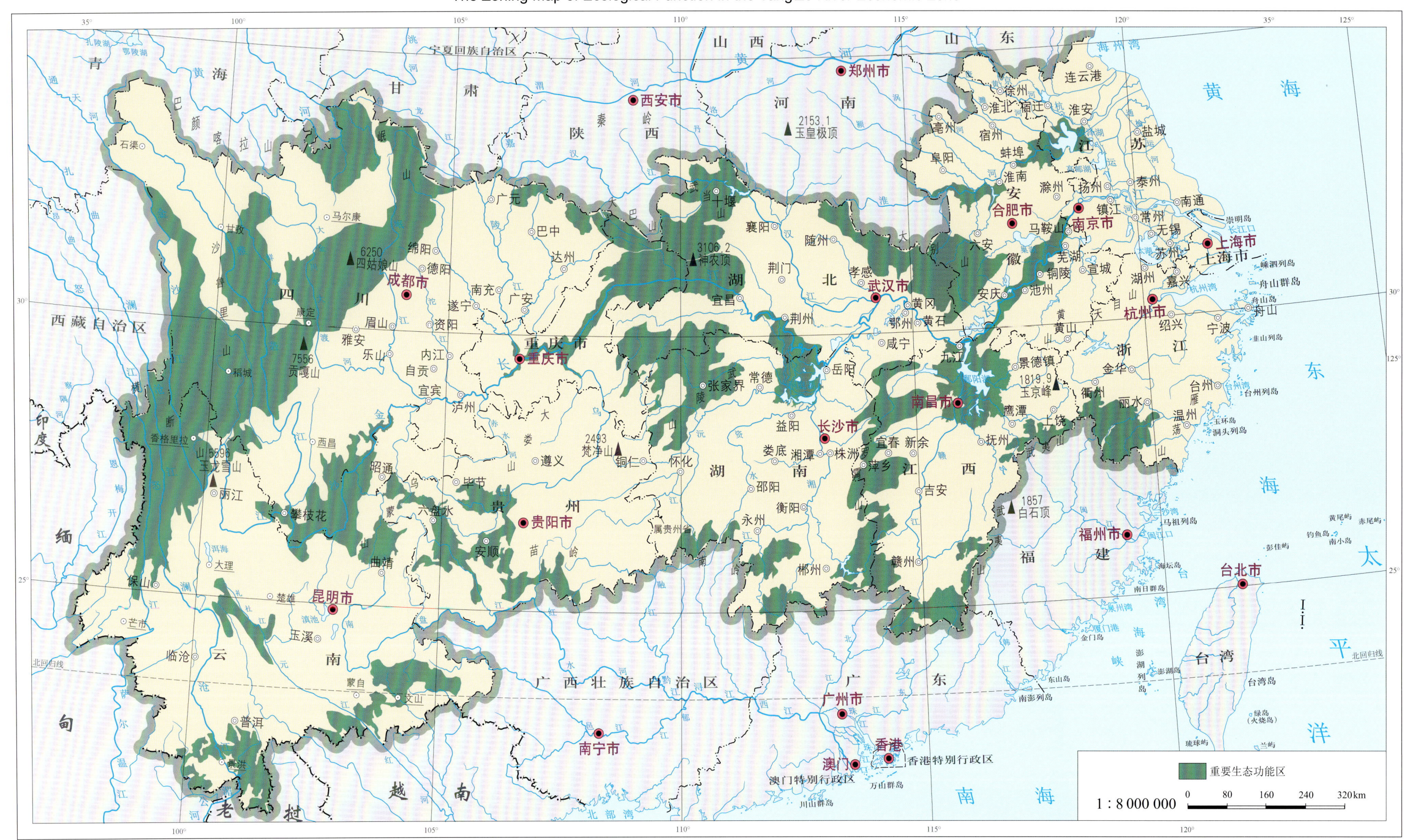

长江经济带重要生态功能区可分为以下4类：①生物多样性维护生态功能区，包括川滇森林及生物多样性生态功能区、秦巴生物多样性生态功能区、南岭山地森林及生物多样性生态功能区、武陵山生物多样性生态功能区；②水土保持生态功能区，包括三峡库区水土保持生态功能区、大别山水土保持生态功能区、武夷山水土保持生态功能区；③重要湿地，包括诺尔盖草原湿地、长江荆江段湿地、淮河中下游湿地、安徽沿江湿地、鄱阳湖湿地；④主要河湖源区，包括珠江源、洞庭湖区、淮河源、赣江-闽江源。

4.4 长江经济带生态用地分布图
The Distribution Map of Ecological Land Utilization in the Yangtze River Economic Zone

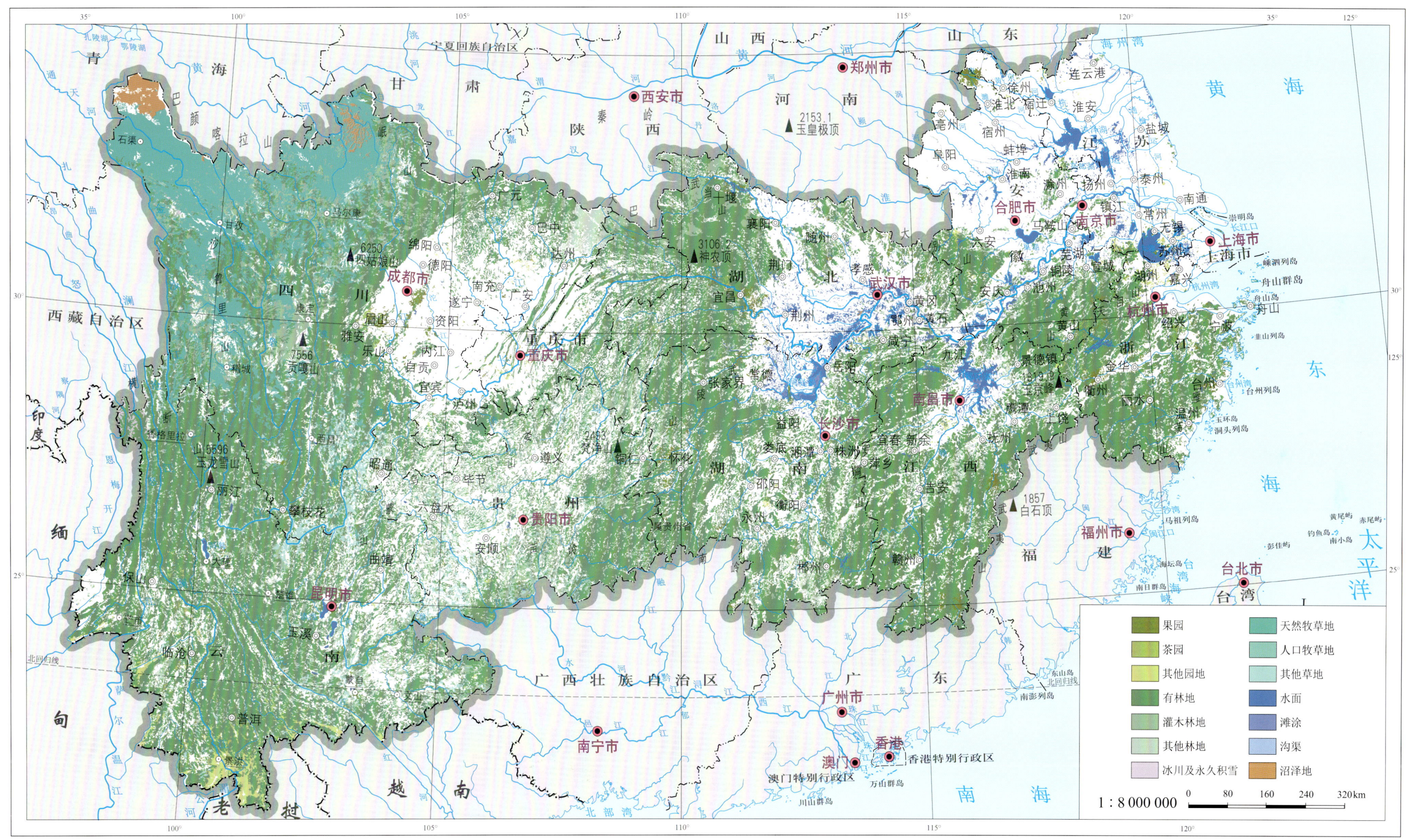

长江经济带耕地类型主要有6类。第一类是林地，除安徽、江苏北部和四川盆地外，均有较集中分布，是最主要的生态用地类型；第二类是草地，主要集中分布在四川西部靠近青藏高原较高海拔地区；第三类是园地，各省均有分布，但比较零散；第四类是水面，主要分布在长江经济带中下游，还包括上游一些河流和湖泊；第五类是滩涂和沼泽，内陆滩涂主要分布在河流、湖泊等水面沿岸周边，沿海滩涂分布在大陆海岸线和海岛岸线，沼泽主要分布在中上游地区；第六类是冰川和永久积雪，均为比较少的生态用地类型，分布于上游高海拔地区。

4.5 长江经济带生态敏感区分布图
The Distribution Map of Ecologically Sensitive Regions in the Yangtze River Economic Zone

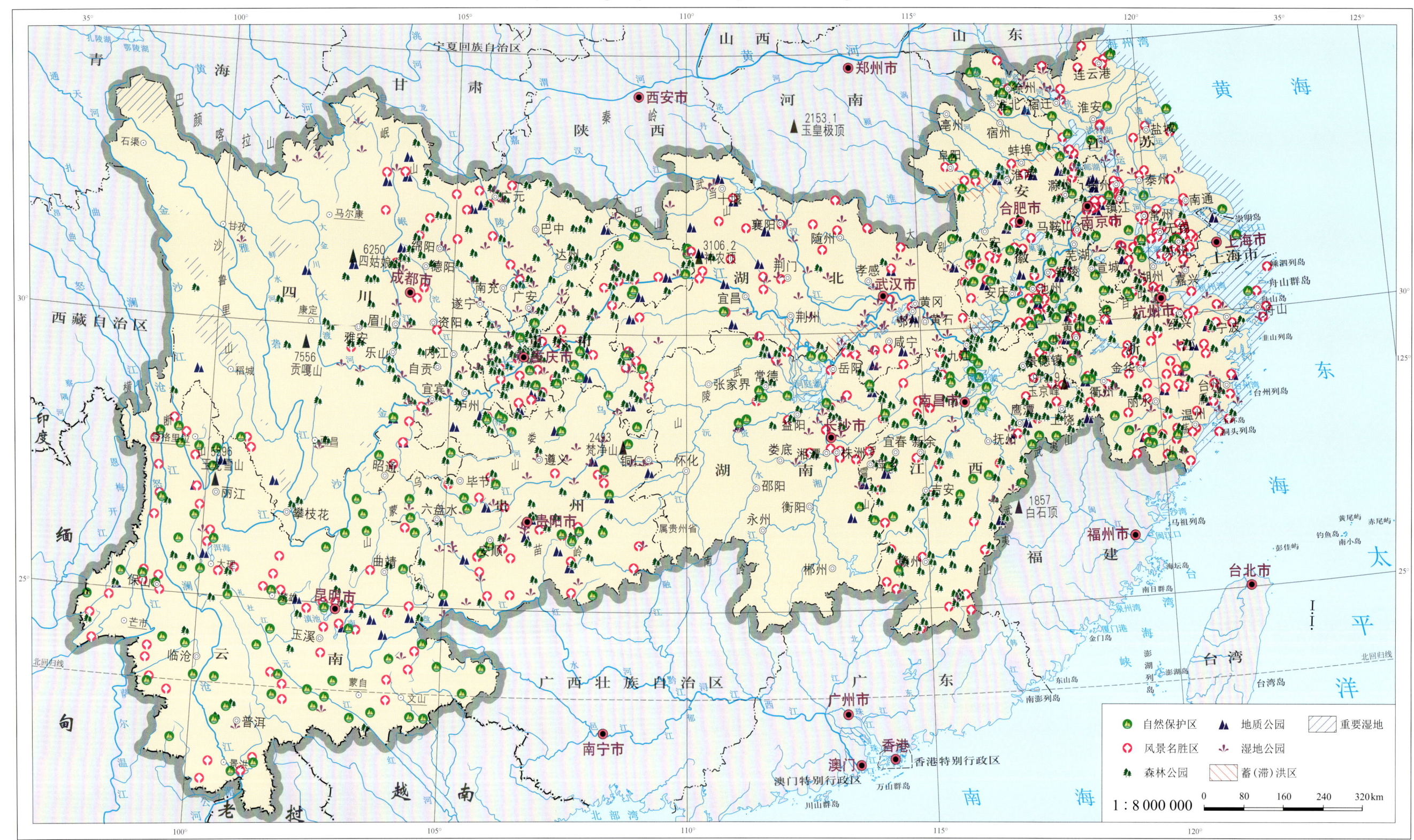

长江经济带有自然保护区1076处，其中国家级123处，省级264处，面积分别为$6.5×10^4 km^2$、$5.8×10^4 km^2$，各省保护区面积占比1.53%~18.54%不等，占比最大的是四川、重庆两省市，占比最小的是江苏、浙江两省。风景名胜区296处，其中国家级223处；森林公园783处，其中国家级162处；地质公园91处，其中世界级地质公园10处。

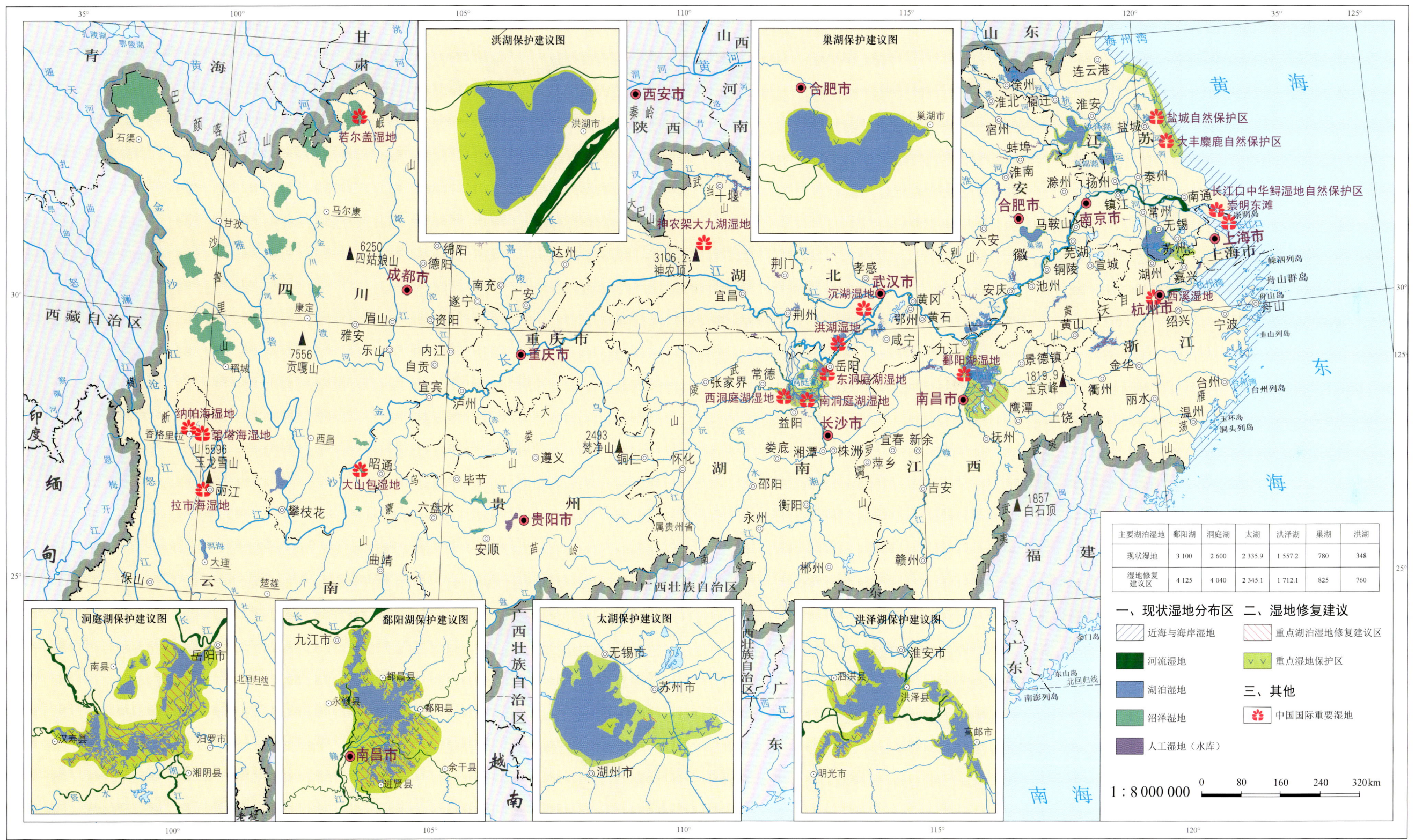

4.7 长三角经济区平原地下水污染状况图
The Groundwater Pollution Status Map of the Plain Area in the Yangtze River Delta Economic Zone

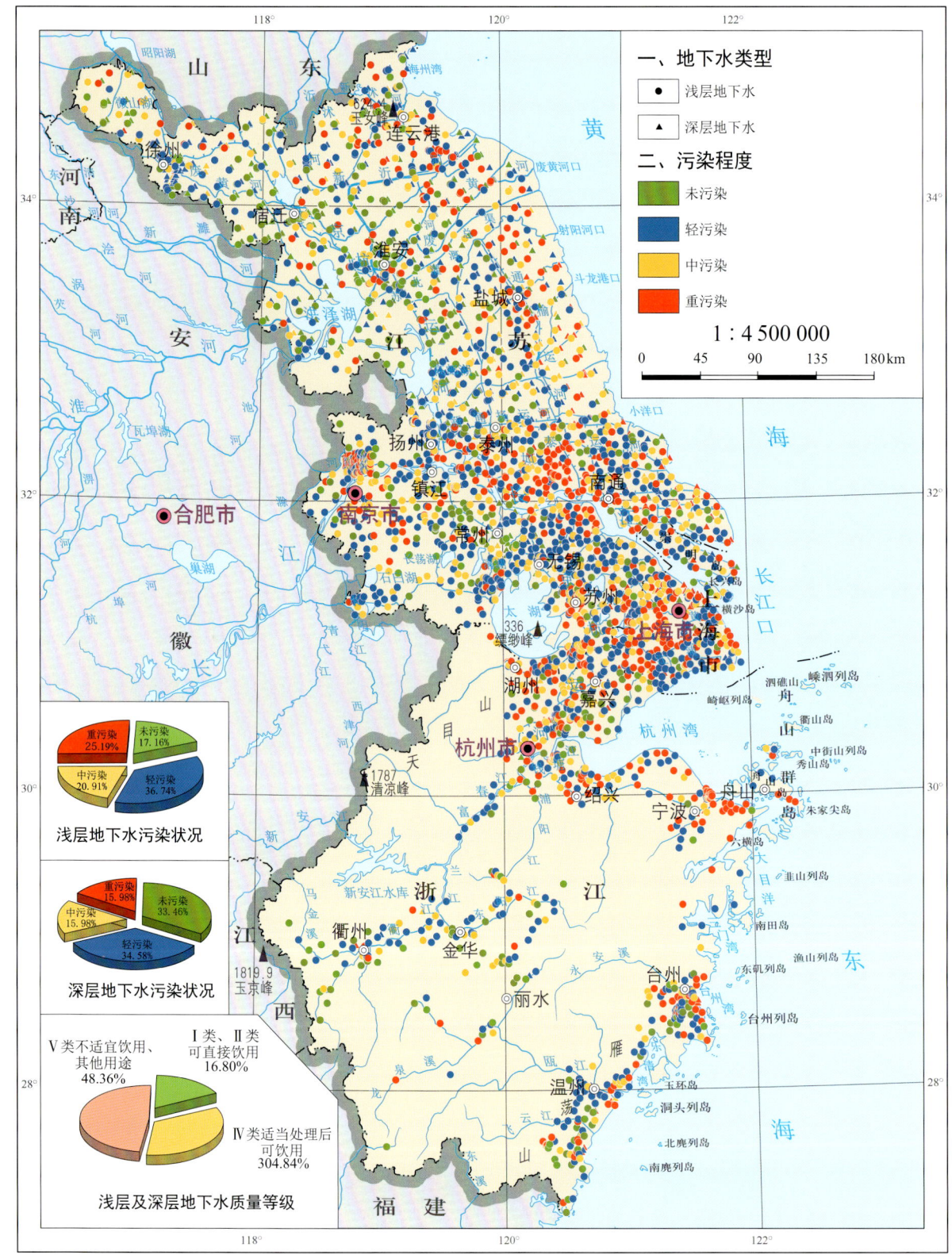

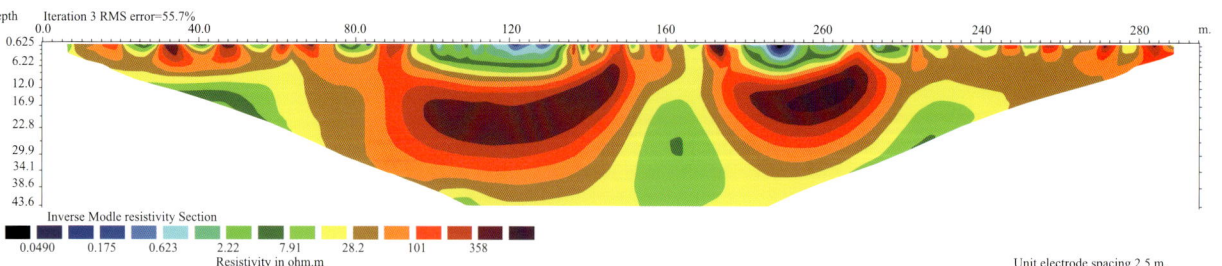

南京燕子矶某化工厂地下含水层污染发黑的岩芯（左上）、现场抽出的污染地下水（右上）与污染晕剖面（下）

浅层地下水重污染样品占25.19%，中污染样品占20.91%，轻污染样品占36.74%，未污染样品占17.16%。深层地下水重污染样品占15.98%，中污染样品占15.98%，轻污染样品占34.58%，未污染样品占33.46%。地下水污染主要是由于工业"三废"无序排放和农业施肥所致。

4.8 长三角经济区平原地下水"三氮"污染状况图
The Trizone Polymers Pollution Map of the Groundwater in the Plain Area of the Yangtze River Delta Economic Zone

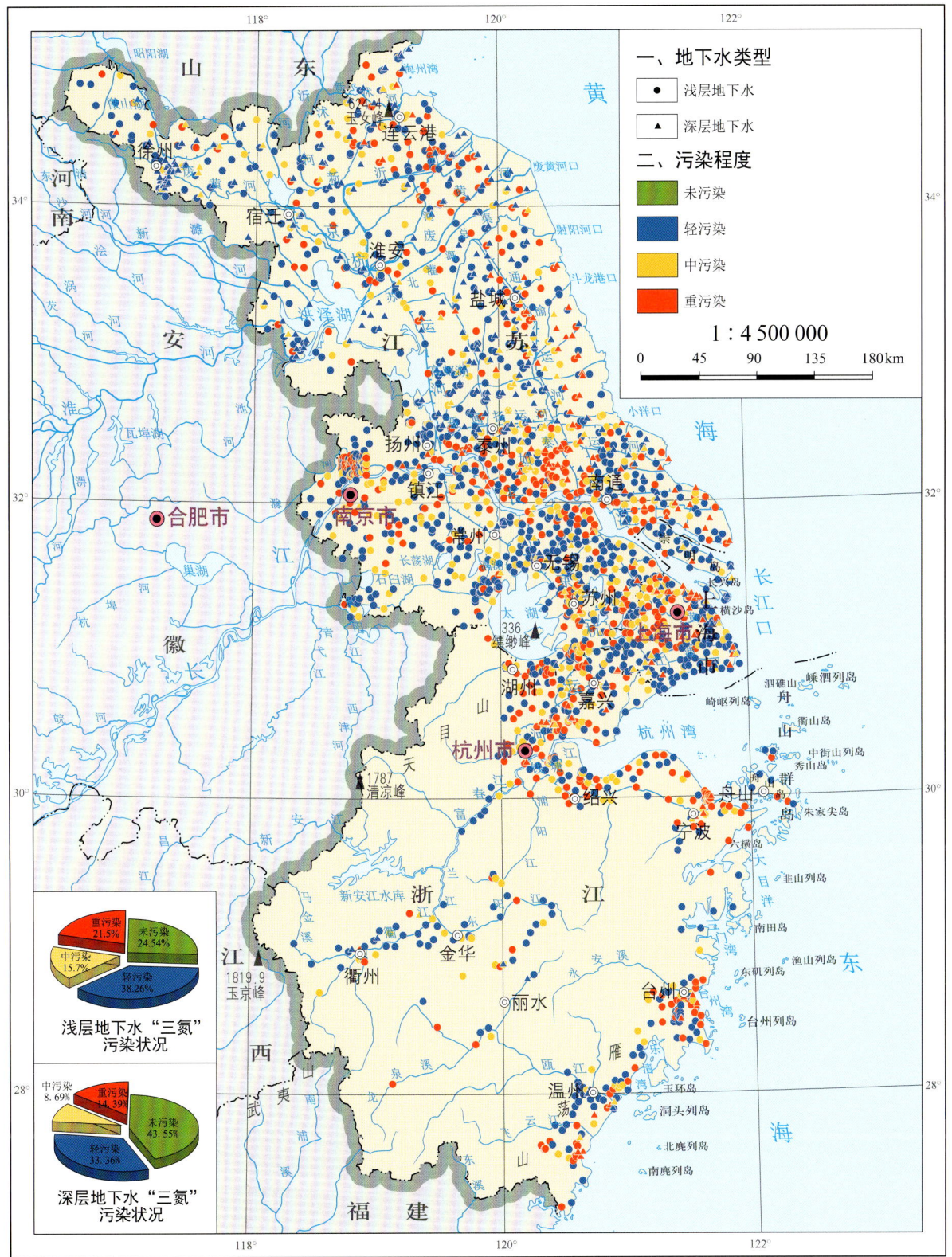

浅层地下水"三氮"污染状况显示：重污染样品占21.50%，全区均有分布，平原多于山区，农村多于城市。深层地下水"三氮"污染状况显示：重污染样品占14.39%，主要分布在长江三角洲北翼、长江口南翼及杭州湾北部，经济发达地区的农业区分布最为广泛。

4.9 长三角经济区平原地下水重金属、有机组分污染图
The Pollution Map of Heavy Metals and Organic Components in the Plain Area of the Yangtze River Delta Economic Zone

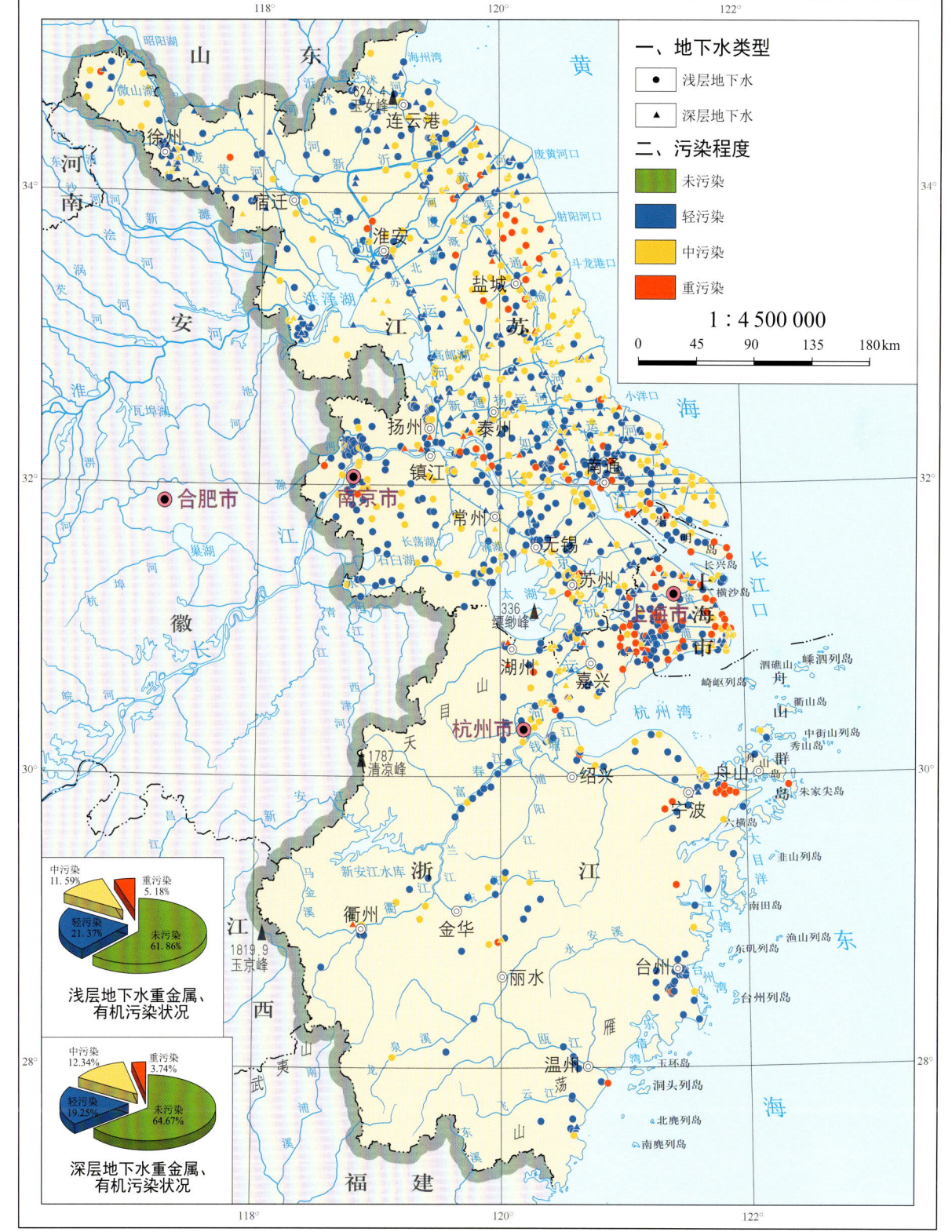

浅层地下水重金属有机污染状况显示：重污染样品占5.18%，相对集中分布于沿江、长江口、上海与昆山、嘉兴结合部。深层地下水重金属有机污染状况显示：重污染样品占3.74%，主要分布于扬州、泰州沿江，南通各县腹地也有少量分布。

4.10 长江经济带二氧化碳地质储存适宜性分区图
The Suitability Zoning Map of Geological Storage for CO₂ in the Yangtze River Economic Zone

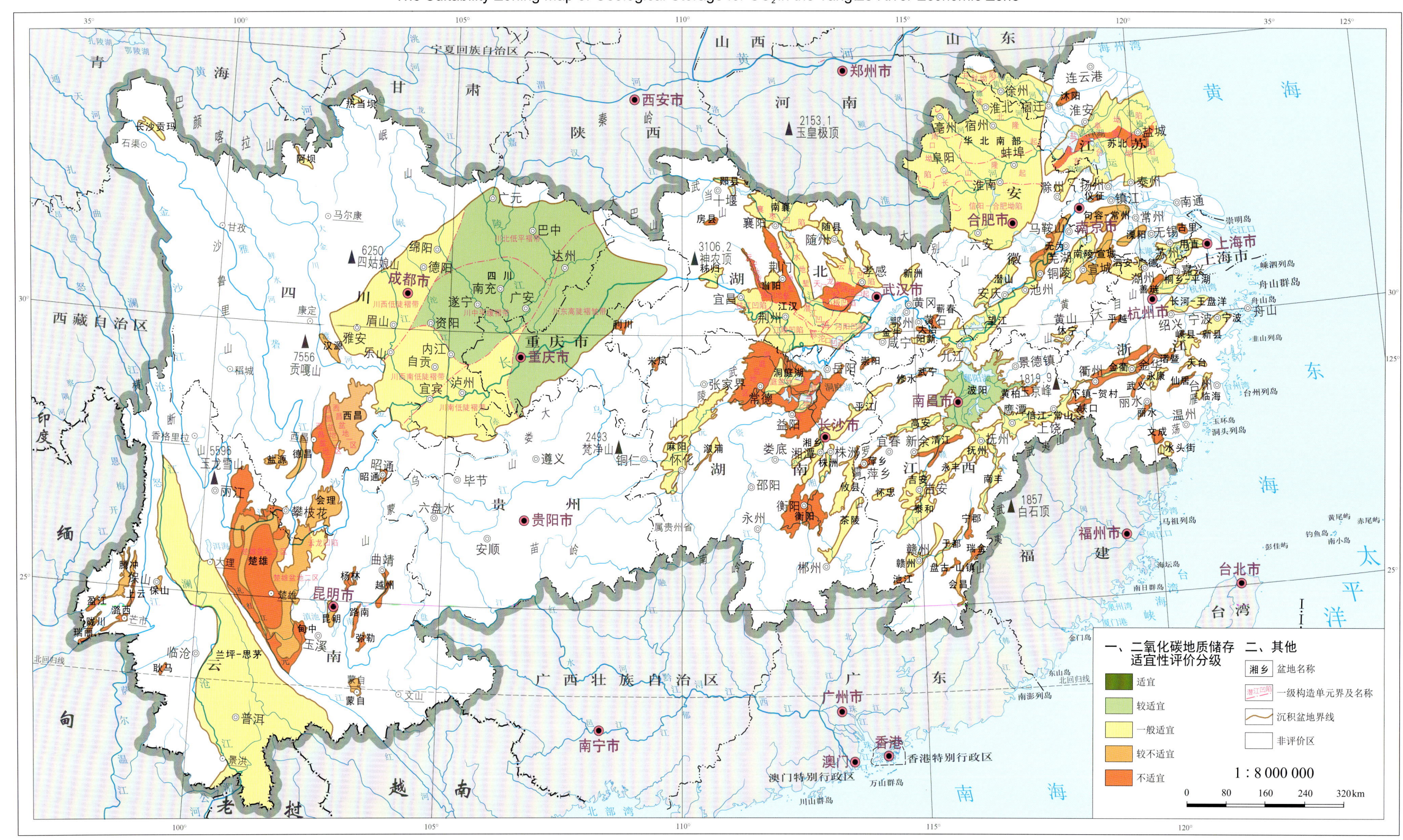

长江经济带沉积盆地总面积约65.1×10⁴km²，二氧化碳地质储存总潜力达90 289×10⁸t。其中深部咸水层储存潜力为823.14×10⁸t，占总潜力的91%；油田储存潜力5.68×10⁸t，占总潜力的1%；气田储存潜力74.07×10⁸t，占总潜力的8%。适宜性评价结果显示，适宜—较适宜储存面积约15.6×10⁴km²，占评价总面积的24%，储存潜力约384×10⁸t，占总储存潜力的42.5%；一般适宜面积约37.2×10⁴km²，占评价总面积的57.1%，储存潜力约495.3×10⁸t，占总储存潜力的54.9%；较不适宜—不适宜面积约12.3×10⁴km²，占评价总面积的18.9%。

5

长江三角洲海岸带地区的国土资源与环境条件

National Land Resources and Environmental Status in Coastal Area along the Yangtze River Delta

5.1 长三角经济区滩涂后备土地资源潜力图
The Back-up Resources Map of Tidal Flat Areas in the Yangtze River Delta Economic Zone

5.2 长三角经济区海域矿产资源分布图
The Distribution Map of Mineral Resources in Sea Area of the Yangtze River Delta Economic Zone

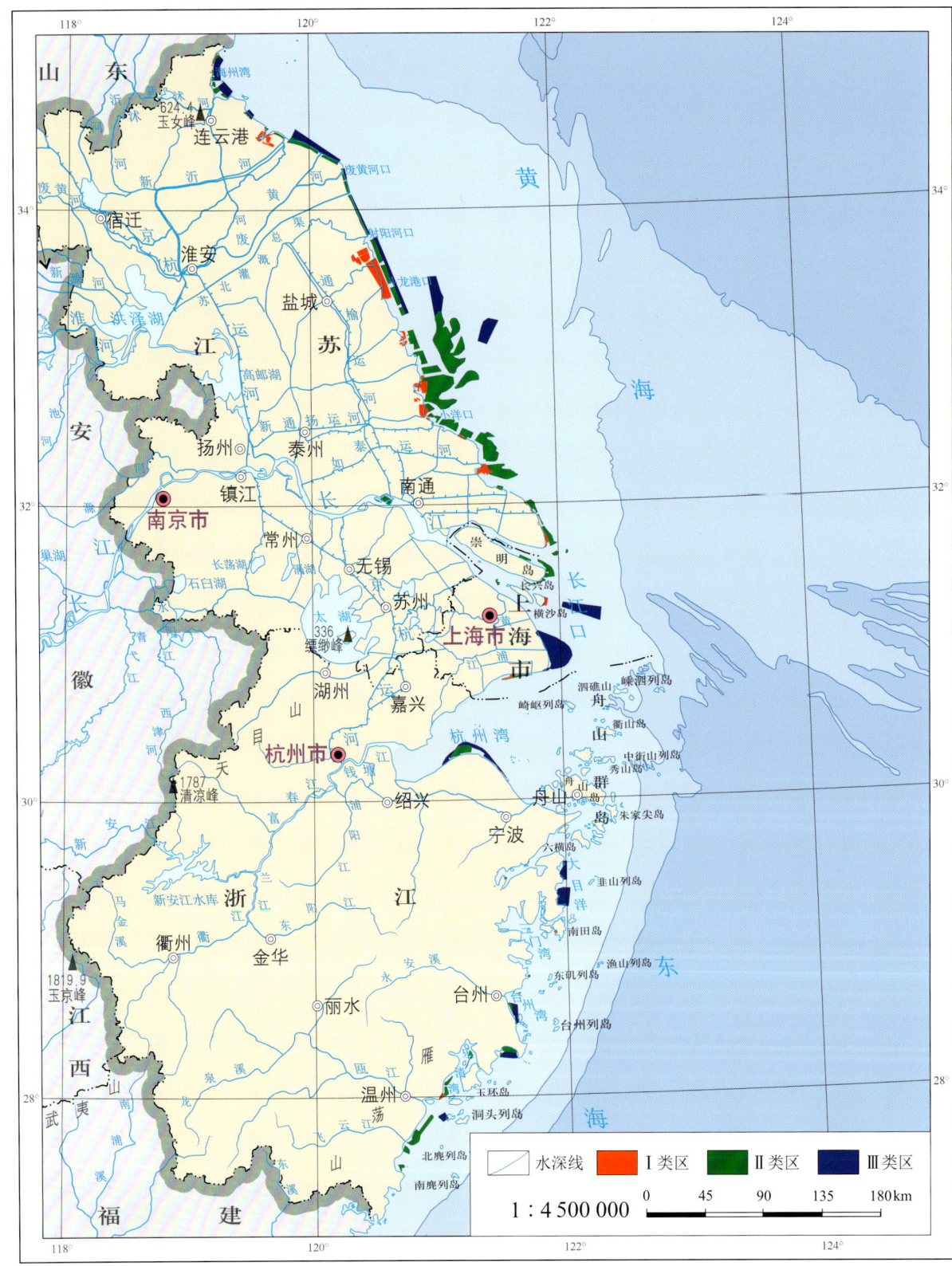

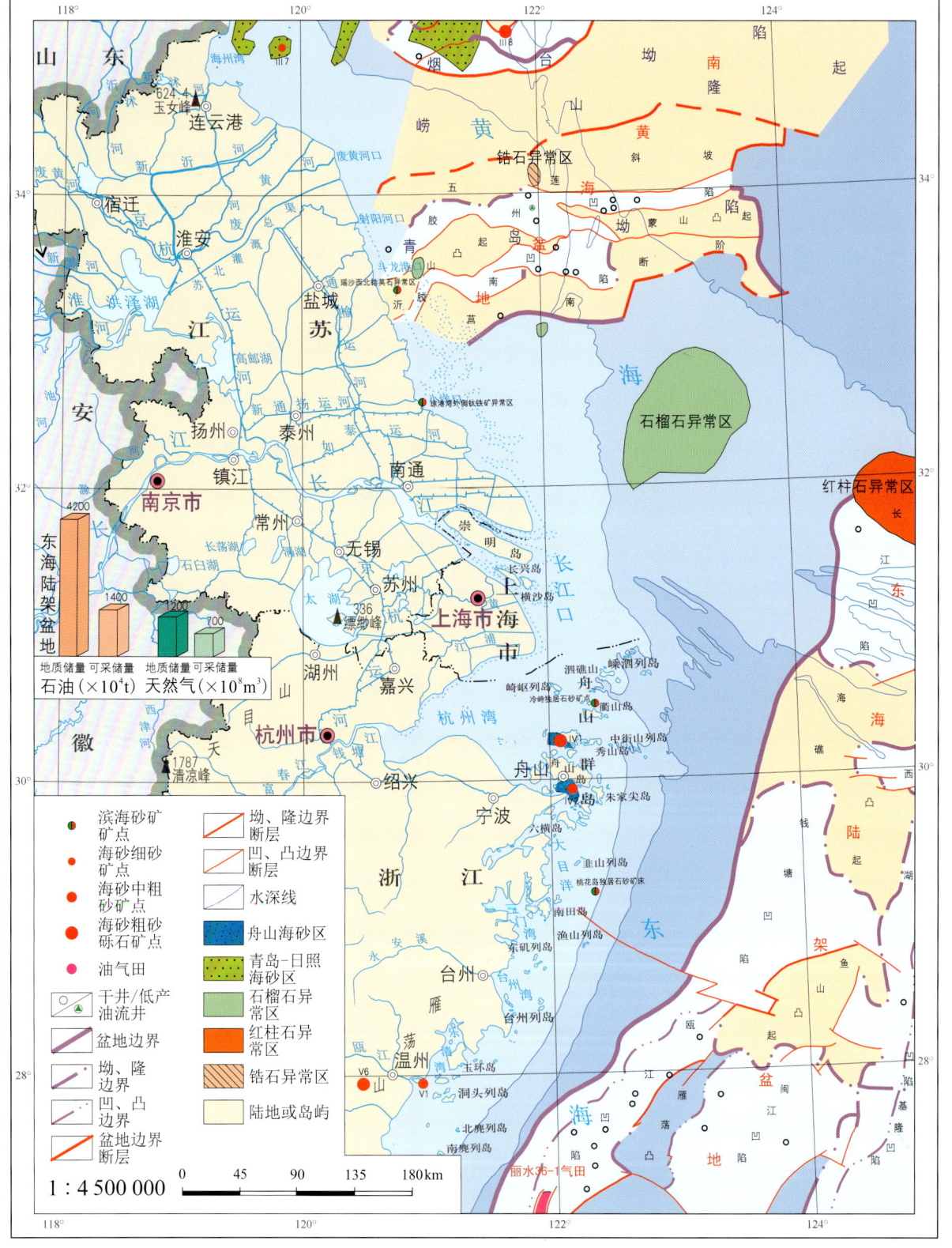

长三角滩涂后备土地资源开发潜力区分为3类：Ⅰ类分布在平均高潮线以上，面积为460km²；Ⅱ类分布在海岸线至最大平均低潮线之间的潮间带滩涂区，最大低潮时普遍出露，面积为3 024km²；Ⅲ类分布在低潮线以外至5m水深浅海域，不能自然出露，面积为2 080km²。

资料显示，南黄海盆地石油地质资源量为$2.98×10^8$t，天然气地质资源量为$1 847×10^8 m^3$；东海陆架盆地石油地质资源量为$7.2×10^8$t，天然气地质资源量为$36×10^{12} m^3$。固体矿产资源以海砂和滨海砂矿为主，其中，舟山海域海砂资源潜力较大，勘查资源量为$6 150×10^4$t。

5.3 长三角经济区海域滨海湿地分布图
The Distribution Map of Coastal Wetlands in the Yangtze River Delta Economic Zone

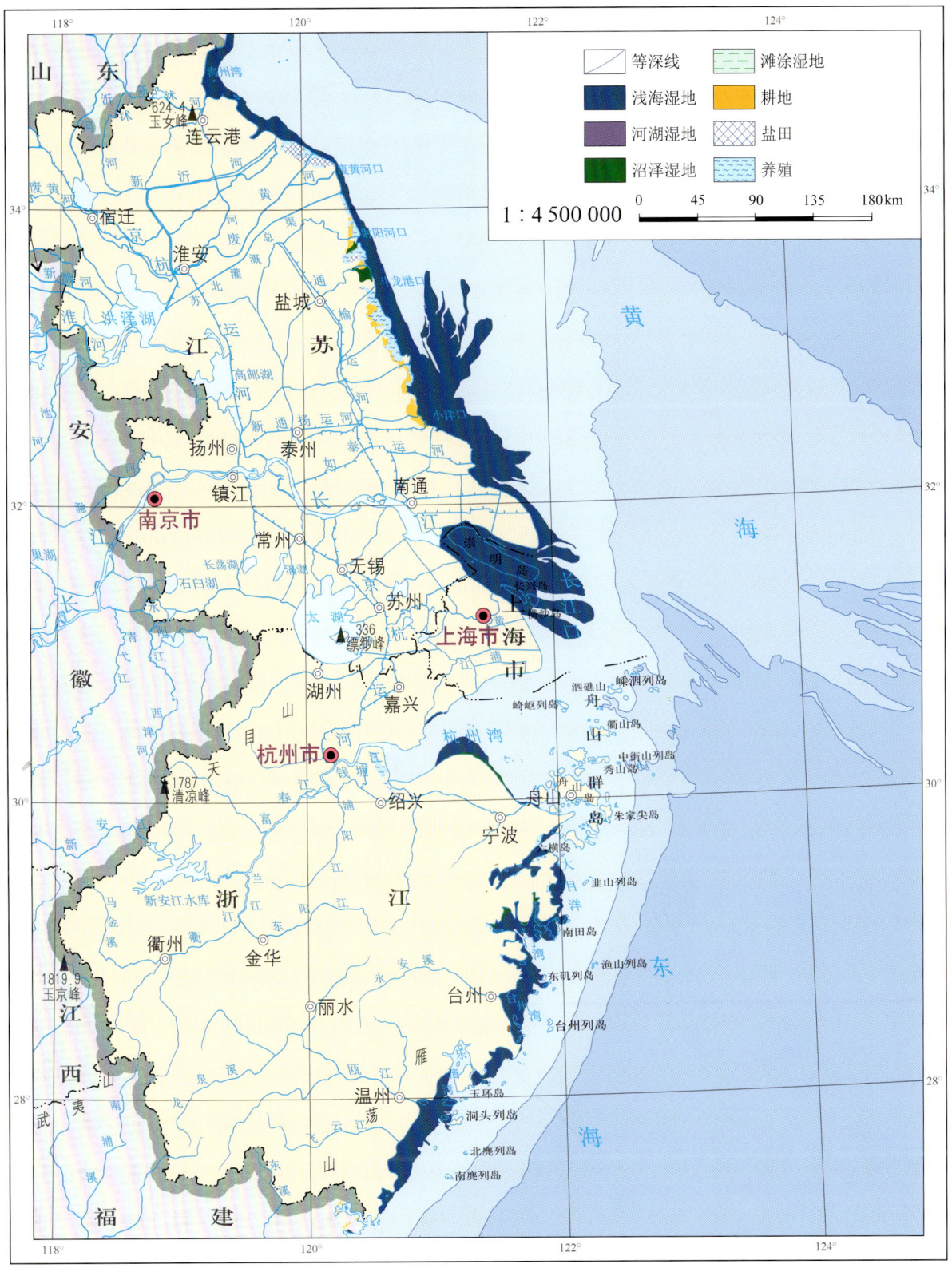

区内拥有丰富的滨海湿地资源，总面积约 $1.323\times10^4 km^2$。江苏拥有亚洲大陆边缘最大海岸型湿地，被列入世界重点湿地保护区，盐城被誉为"东方湿地之都"。沿岸开发建设及滩涂围垦对滨海湿地构成严重威胁，存在环境污染加重、外来物种入侵及潮滩侵淤等问题。

5.4 长三角经济区海域水深地形图
The Bathyorographical Map of Sea Area in the Yangtze River Delta Economic Zone

区内拥有世界上最大河口三角洲之一的长江三角洲，最大潮流沉积体系之一的苏北潮流沙脊群和东海陆架潮流沙脊群。水下地形总体平缓，舟山群岛附近海域地形变化急剧，江苏辐射沙脊群由10多条数十千米至近百千米放射状沙脊组成，多数沙脊近岸部分低潮时出露。

附 件

支撑服务长江经济带发展地质调查报告（2015年）

——长江经济带建设需关注的四大有利资源环境条件和四个重大地质问题

为支撑服务长江经济带发展战略，国土资源部中国地质调查局会同长江经济带11省（市）国土资源部门，系统梳理了以往地质调查成果，对长江经济带资源环境条件和重大地质问题进行了研究。初步研究结果表明，长江经济带耕地、页岩气、地热、锂等资源条件优越，4.5亿亩（1亩＝666.67m²）无重金属污染耕地集中分布，拥有3个国家级页岩气勘查开发基地，探明储量$5441×10^8m^3$，每年地热可利用量折合标准煤$2.4×10^8t$，相当于2014年燃煤量的19%，发现亚洲最大的能源金属矿床，资源环境条件有利于发展现代农业、清洁能源产业和战略新兴产业。长江经济带活动断裂、岩溶塌陷、地面沉降、滑坡、崩塌、泥石流等重大地质问题，影响过江通道、高速铁路和城市群规划建设，12条拟建的过江通道地质适宜性较差，沪昆高铁19%线路存在地质安全隐患。同时，耕地酸化、地下水污染、矿山环境地质问题比较突出，影响绿色生态廊道建设，应予以关注。

6.1 支撑长江经济带发展的四大有利资源环境条件

长江经济带无重金属污染的耕地资源丰富，页岩气、地热等新型清洁能源开发利用前景好，锂、稀土、钒钛、钨锡等战略矿产资源储量大，有利于支撑长江经济带发展。

（1）长江经济带无重金属污染耕地4.5亿亩，绿色富硒耕地1836万亩，有利于现代农业和特色农业发展。

长江经济带耕地总面积6.8亿亩，占全国的33.4%。根据已完成的5.4亿亩耕地质量地球化学调查结果，耕地环境质量总体良好，无重金属污染耕地约4.5亿亩（见附表1），占已调查面积的83.3%，主要分布在四川盆地、江汉平原、鄱阳湖平原、巢湖平原、洞庭湖平原和太湖平原等地区。拟将无重金属污染耕地优先划入永久基本农田，打造粮食生产核心区和主要农产品优势区。

调查发现绿色富硒耕地1836万亩（见附表1，附图1），主要分布于成都平原、江汉平原、鄱阳湖平原、太湖平原和金衢盆地等地区。湖南、湖北、江西、安徽、浙江等省富硒耕地面积均在200万亩以上。建议推广江西丰城、湖北恩施等地区富硒耕地开发经验，科学规划和合理利用绿色富硒耕地资源，打造一批富硒产业园或名特优农产品产业基地。

（2）长江经济带页岩气可采资源量$15.5×10^{12}m^3$，占全国的62%，有利于打造清洁低碳能源产业带。

长江经济带页岩气资源潜力巨大，可采资源量$15.5×10^{12}m^3$，占全国的62%。目前我国页岩气探明地质储量$5441×10^8m^3$，集中分布在长江经济带的重庆涪陵、四川长宁—威远、云南昭通等地。重庆涪陵探明页岩气地质储量$3806×10^8m^3$，已建成我国第一个页岩气开发基地，年产能$35×10^8m^3$。

2017年，国土资源部中国地质调查局在财政部的支持下，页岩气调查取得了一系列重大发现和重要进展。湖北宜昌页岩气调查钻获70m厚优质含页岩层，显示该区页岩气资源潜力大。贵州遵义天然气调查有重大发现，钻获两个厚层含油气新层系，预示着下伏页岩具有较好的含气性，将带动整个南方新区新层系天然气和页岩气勘查。鄂西秭归和湘西慈利部署实施的页岩气调查也取得了重要进展。拟加大页岩气资源调查和勘查力度，组织开展第三轮页岩气勘查区块招标，引入更多有资格条件和经济技术实力的市场主体参与页岩气勘查开发，加快推进重庆涪陵等3个国家级页岩气综合开发示范区建设，加快技术创新，推动页岩气相关产业发展。

（3）长江经济带浅层地温能和热水型地热资源丰富，每年可利用热量折合标准煤$2.4×10^8t$，相当于2014年燃煤量的19%，有利于促进城市节能减排和地热相关产业发展。

调查评价表明，长江经济带11个省会城市规划区浅层地温能潜力巨大，每年可利用热量折合标准煤$2.0×10^8t$。若采用地源热泵系统充分开发利用浅层地温能，每年可实现夏季制冷面积$24.6×10^8m^2$，冬季供暖面积$44.2×10^8m^2$，可减排二氧化碳$1.66×10^8t$。目前，11个省会城市均有浅层地温能利用工程，共计720处，供热制冷面积超过$900×10^4m^2$，经济和社会效益显著。热水型地热资源主要分布在四川盆地、江汉盆地、苏北盆地、淮北平原和川西、滇西山区（见附图2），每年可采地热水$69.3×10^8m^3$，可利用热量折合标准煤$0.4×10^8t$，目前每年利用量仅为1.2%。建议加大浅层地温能和热水型地热资源等公益性地质勘查，降低商业勘查风险，并通过价格补贴、税收优惠等政策鼓励推进开发利用，支撑地热供暖制冷、温室养殖和温泉旅游等产业发展。

（4）长江经济带锂、稀土等战略矿产资源储量大，有利于推进新材料、高端制造、新能源汽车等新兴产业发展。

长江经济带稀土、钛等矿产储量占全国的80%以上，锂、钨、锡、钒资源储量占全国的50%以上。四川甲基卡发现亚洲最大的能源金属锂矿床，探明资源储量$188×10^4t$。安徽金寨发现特大钼矿床，资源储量$246×10^4t$，属亚洲第一、世界第二。重稀土储量大，居世界前列，主要分布在江西赣州、湖南岳阳等地。钒钛探明储量$6.6×10^8t$，主要分布在四川、湖南等地。钨锡探明储量$650×10^4t$，主要分布在江西、湖南、云南。建议充分利用锂、钼、稀土、钒钛、钨锡等战略矿产资源，推进锂电池、火箭和热核反应燃料、特种合金、超导材料、航空航天工业等战略性新兴产业发展。

6.2 长江经济带发展需要关注的4个重大地质问题

长江经济带横跨东、中、西三大地势阶梯，地貌单元多样，地质条件复杂，活动断裂、岩溶塌陷、滑坡、崩塌、泥石流灾害、地面沉降等地质问题突出。调查表明，区内主要活动断裂带94条（见附图3），岩溶塌陷高易发区$23.5×10^4km^2$（见附图4），滑坡、崩塌、泥石流灾害隐患点10.7万余处（见附图5），地面沉降严重区约$2×10^4km^2$，过江通道、高速铁路、重要城市群等规划建设应对这些重大地质问题予以高度关注。

（1）规划的95条过江通道中，83条地质适宜性良好，12条地质适宜性较差，建议针对活动断裂、岩溶塌陷等地质问题，进一步开展地质勘查，合理确定通道位置和过江方式。

根据活动断裂、岩溶塌陷对过江通道安全的影响，初步评价了过江通道位置地质适宜性。评价结果表明，规划的95条过江通道中，83条通道位置地质适宜性良好，12条通道位置地质适宜性较差（见附表2，附图6）。其中，江苏常泰、湖北武穴、四川白塔山等9条通道位置受活动断裂影响，湖北武汉地铁11号线、嘉鱼、赤壁等3条通道位置存在岩溶塌陷隐患。建议在过江通道规划建设中，针对相应问题进一步开展地质勘查，合理确定过江通道的具体位置。

从工程建设的地质适宜性角度，对95条通道的过江方式进行了初步比选。长江上游（宜昌以上）的48条过江通道位于河道深切、河床卵砾石层厚的江段，不利于隧道施工，同时，基岩埋藏浅、江岸稳定，有利于大桥建设，宜采用桥梁方式。综合考虑河道切割深度、河床沉积物厚度、及均一性、河流深水线位置、江岸稳定性等因素，长江中下游27条过江通道宜采用桥梁方式，12条宜采用隧道方式，8条采用桥梁和隧道方式均可（见附表3）。建议进一步勘查河道水下地形、水文条件、河床沉积物工程地质与岸线稳定性条件，结合施工工艺和交通状况，合理确定通道过江方式。

（2）沪昆高铁线路有434km存在地质安全隐患，建议加强监测预警与防控；沪汉蓉高铁南京—安庆段、武汉—万州段规划选线应高度关注岩溶塌陷和软土沉降等问题。

沪昆高速铁路全线长度2 264km，穿越长江中下游平原、湘赣丘陵山地、云贵高原等地貌单元，有434km线路存在地质安全隐患。沪昆高铁嘉兴段有24km穿越地面沉降区，近年监测表明，虽然整体沉降趋缓，但局部年沉降量仍大于10mm，建议加强地下水位变化与地面沉降监测。江西樟树—萍乡、湖南湘潭—娄底、贵州普安—盘县等路段岩溶发育，煤矿集中分布，采煤大量抽排地下水，容易诱发地面塌陷，影响392km高铁运营安全，建议加强高铁沿线煤矿区地下水抽排引起的地下水位和地面塌陷变形监测。

云南嵩明段活动断裂发育，有18km穿越Ⅸ～Ⅹ度地震烈度区，历史上多次发生地震，1833年地震震级达8级，建议做好工程防震减震措施和运营期地震微动监测。

拟建的沪汉蓉沿江高速铁路，南京至安庆段、武汉至万州段规划选线时，应高度关注岩溶塌陷、软土沉降等地质问题。南京至安庆段，长江南岸繁昌—铜陵—池州一带岩溶分布面积1 780km²，已发生岩溶塌陷超过100处，同时，长江南岸软土大范围连续分布，面积4 900km²，而长江北岸和县—无为—安庆一带地质条件良好，建议规划优先选择南京—无为—安庆线路方案。武汉至万州段，潜江—荆州—枝江一带软土问题严重，软土层厚度大于5m的线路绵延190km；天门—荆门一带存在大范围岩溶和采空塌陷，面积2 400km²；而天门—当阳一带基岩埋藏浅，路基稳定性好，建议规划优先选择武汉—天门—当阳—万州线路。

（3）长三角、长江中游、成渝城市群面临的主要地质问题分别是地面沉降、岩溶塌陷和滑坡、崩塌、泥石流灾害，建议加强城镇地质安全风险评价，科学规划城镇布局。

长三角城市群经历了城镇化蔓延式发展阶段，地下水严重超采，导致了严重的区域地面沉降。上海、苏锡常、杭嘉湖等地区地面沉降严重，累计沉降量大于200mm的沉降区面积接近1×10⁴km²，经多年防治，已得到了有效控制，沉降速率趋缓，2014年沉降量普遍低于7mm。但是，在江苏盐城、大丰等地新发现地面沉降现象，且呈发展态势，累计沉降量大于200mm的沉降区面积超过1×10⁴km²（见附表4），2014年最大沉降量超过25mm。建议合理调控上海、苏锡常、杭嘉湖等地面沉降趋缓区地下水开采，严格限制江苏沿海地面沉降加剧区地下水开采，进一步加强地面沉降监测预警和风险管控。

长江中游城市群城镇化主要面临岩溶塌陷问题。调查表明，岩溶塌陷高易发区主要分布于武汉市、黄石—鄂州沿江地区、瑞昌—九江—彭泽沿江地区、乐平—丰城—萍乡一带、湖南宁乡等地，19个城市规划建设区受到岩溶塌陷影响，面积达4 700km²（见附表5）。武汉市受岩溶塌陷威胁最为严重，近10年发生岩溶塌陷23处，其中，17处为桩基施工或地下水疏排诱发。建议加强城镇建设用地岩溶塌陷风险分区评价，加强岩溶塌陷防治和监测预警，规范工程建设施工。

成渝城市群（见附图7）城镇化主要面临地震、滑坡、崩塌、泥石流灾害问题。都江堰、石棉、宝兴等24个县（市）多个重要城镇沿龙门山断裂带、荣经-盐津断裂带分布，受地震影响较大，汉源、屏山、云阳、万州等26个县级以上城市位于四川盆地周边山区，存在滑坡、崩塌、泥石流灾害隐患（见附表6）。建议适当控制活动断裂影响区城镇人口规模，科学开展区内城镇规划建设，加强川西、渝东北等山区城镇地质灾害风险评价、监测预警和综合治理。

（4）生态廊道建设需要高度关注耕地酸化和地下水污染、矿山地质环境破坏等问题，建议采取措施抑制耕地酸化，加强地下水管护，推进矿业转型升级和绿色矿山建设。

调查表明，长江经济带酸性耕地面积2.3亿亩，占已调查面积43%，主要分布于江西、湖南、宁波—台州沿海和金华衢州盆地等地。与第二次全国土壤普查资料的对比表明，部分地区耕地酸化趋势明显。酸化会引起耕地重金属的活化，导致养分元素的淋失，影响耕地的耕作性能。建议加强酸性物质污染排放和酸性化肥施用的管控，抑制耕地酸化趋势，实施休耕轮作，促使耕地质量状况好转。

调查表明，长江经济带地下水中氮污染和重金属污染较重，有机污染凸显，污染样品超标率达17%。地下水氮污染以硝酸盐和氨氮为主，氮污染超标率14.1%，主要分布在农业区。汞、镉、铬等重金属污染超标率3.5%，零星分布在城市周边及工矿企业周围。四氯化碳等有毒有害有机污染物超标率为0.6%，多呈点状分布在工业区及其附近。建议着力做好水源区、城镇及其周边等重点地区地下水污染防控，坚持以防为主，以自然修复为主，监测预警与工程治理相结合，遏制地下水水质恶化趋势。

长江经济带现有矿山5.4万多座，铁、锰、铅、锌等金属矿多为小规模分散开采，大中型矿山仅占7%，低于全国10%的平均水平。传统开发利用方式破坏矿山地质环境严重，截至2014年，累计损毁土地约5 000km²，固体废弃物存量达84×10⁸t，年排放废水超过27×10⁸m³。建议推进矿业集约发展和转型升级，加强14个大型矿产资源基地建设（见附表7、附图8）；尽快建成227处国家级绿色矿山示范区，大力开展绿色矿山建设，改善矿山地质环境，实现矿地和谐。

6.3 "十三五"支撑服务长江经济带发展地质工作设想

"十三五"期间，国土资源部中国地质调查局将全面贯彻落实十八届五中全会精神和《中共中央关于制定国民经济和社会发展第十三个五年规划的建议》中关于推进长江经济带发展战略的要求，以支撑服务黄金水道功能提升、立体交通走廊建设、产业转型升级、新型城镇化建设、绿色生态廊道打造等重大任务为目标，以研究解决影响和制约长江经济带发展的重大地质问题为导向，开展长江经济带地质调查，主要部署在"4个经济区"（长三角、皖江、长江中游和成渝）、"3条发展线"（沿江、沿海和高铁沿线）和"4个重点区"（重大工程区、重要成矿区、重大问题区和重要生态区），包括6个方面工作：一是围绕新型城镇化战略，开展长三角、长江中游、成渝等城市群环境地质调查；二是围绕产业转型升级，开展长江中下游、西南三江、湘西鄂西等重要成矿带矿产资源调查和川渝、鄂西、滇黔等地区页岩气资源调查；三是围绕重大工程和重大基础设施建设，开展沿江、沿海和沿高铁发展带工程地质调查；四是围绕重大地质问题，开展长江中上游地区岩溶塌陷调查、主要断裂带活动断裂调查、上游山区城镇滑坡、崩塌、泥石流调查；五是围绕现代农业发展，开展中西部地区1:25万和东部地区1:5万耕地质量地球化学调查；六是围绕生态廊道建设，开展丹江口库区、鄱阳湖地区、三峡库区等生态脆弱区环境地质调查。

为加快推进长江经济带地质调查工作，国土资源部中国地质调查局将联合长江经济带11省（市）国土资源部门召开"长江经济带地质调查工作研讨会"，创新构建中央和地方地质工作联动协调机制，在财政部的支持下，按照中央与地方事权、财权划分的原则，每年拟安排中央财政经费12亿元，统筹地方财政资金，共同推进地质调查工作，构建国土资源环境承载力评价与监测预警体系，更加有力地支撑服务长江经济带发展战略。

附图1　长江经济带无重金属污染和富硒耕地分布图

附图2 长江经济带地热资源分布图

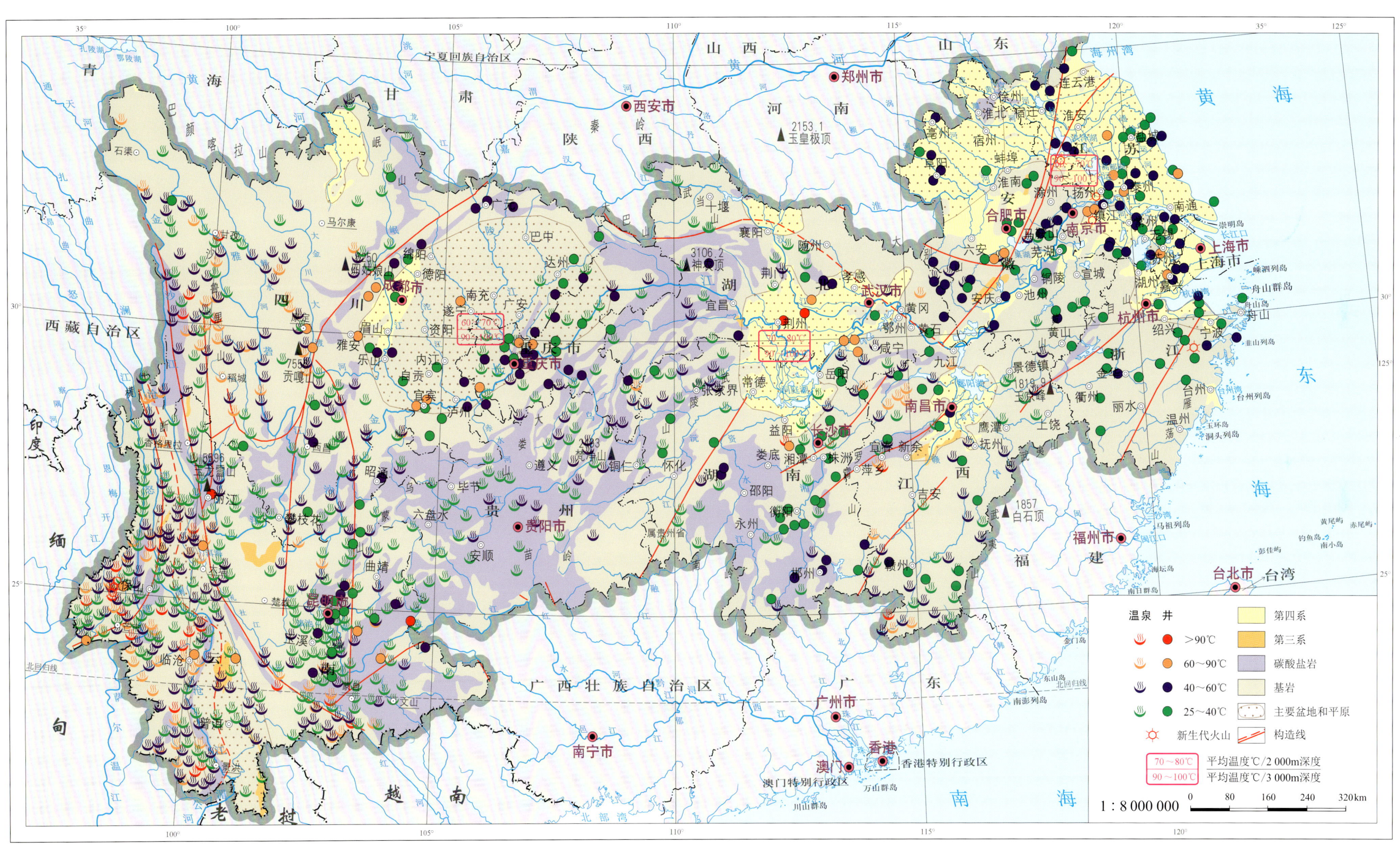

附图3 长江经济带活动断裂与地震分布图

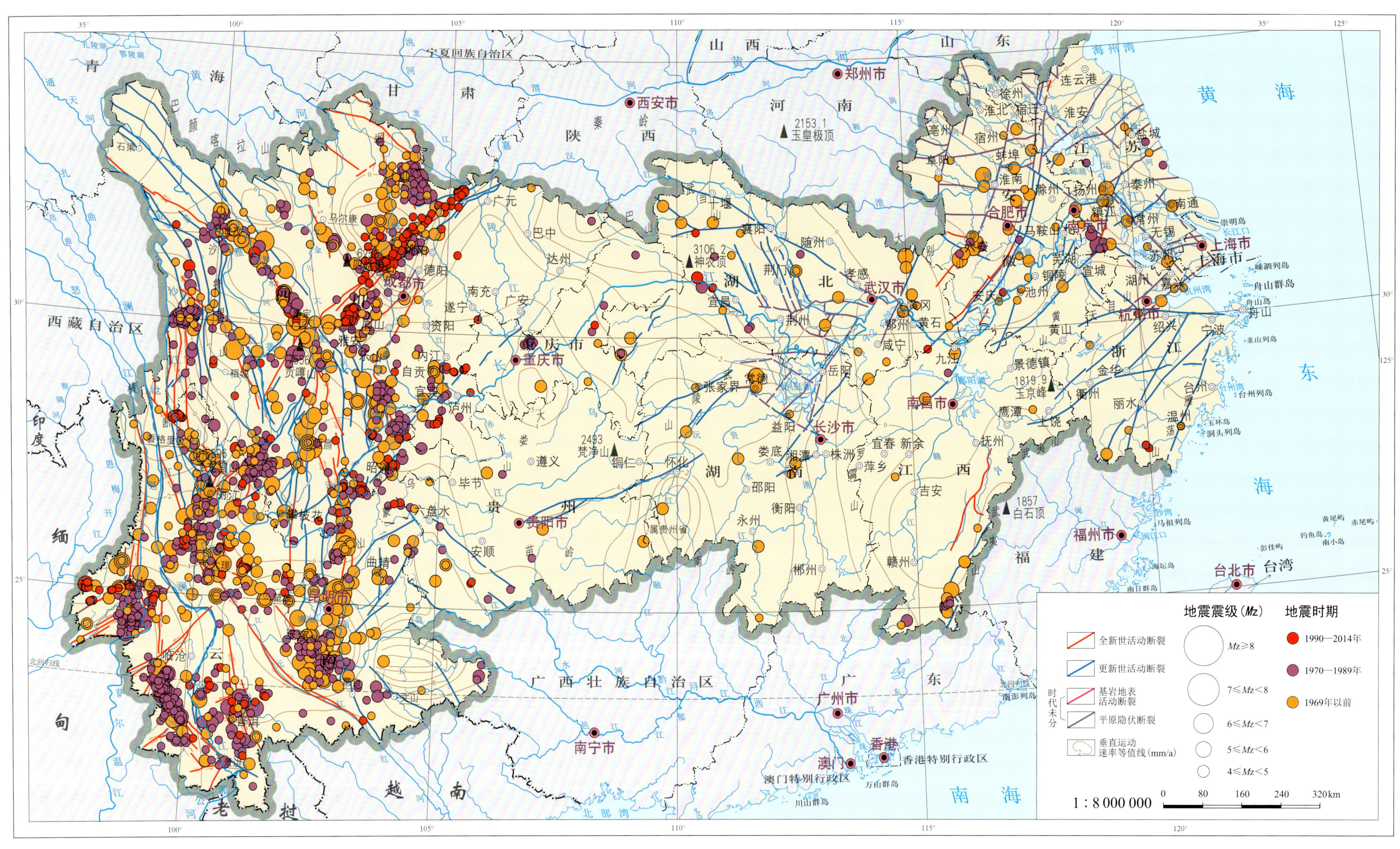

附图4 长江经济带岩溶塌陷易发性评价图

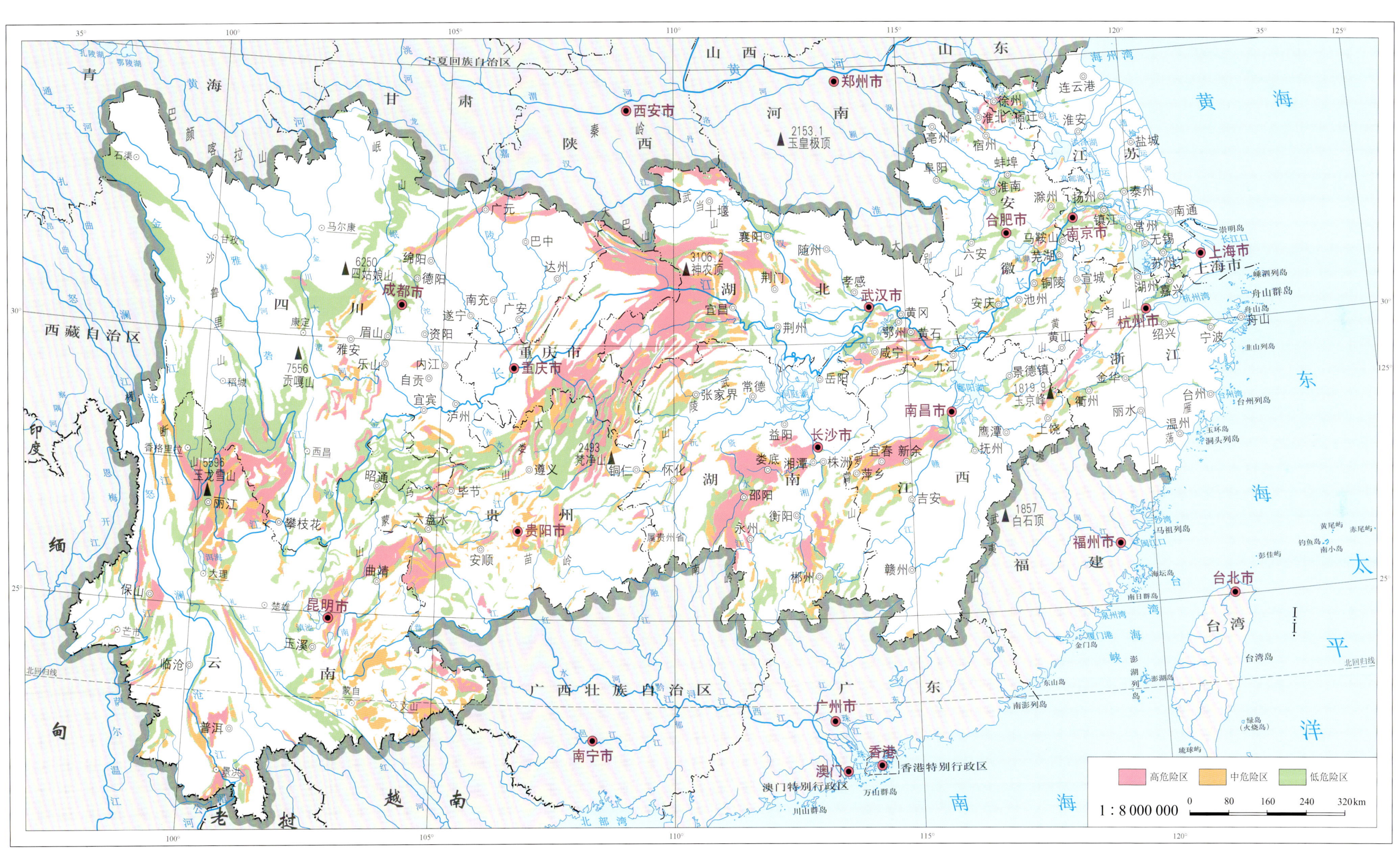

附图5　长江经济带滑坡、崩塌、泥石流分布及易发性评价图

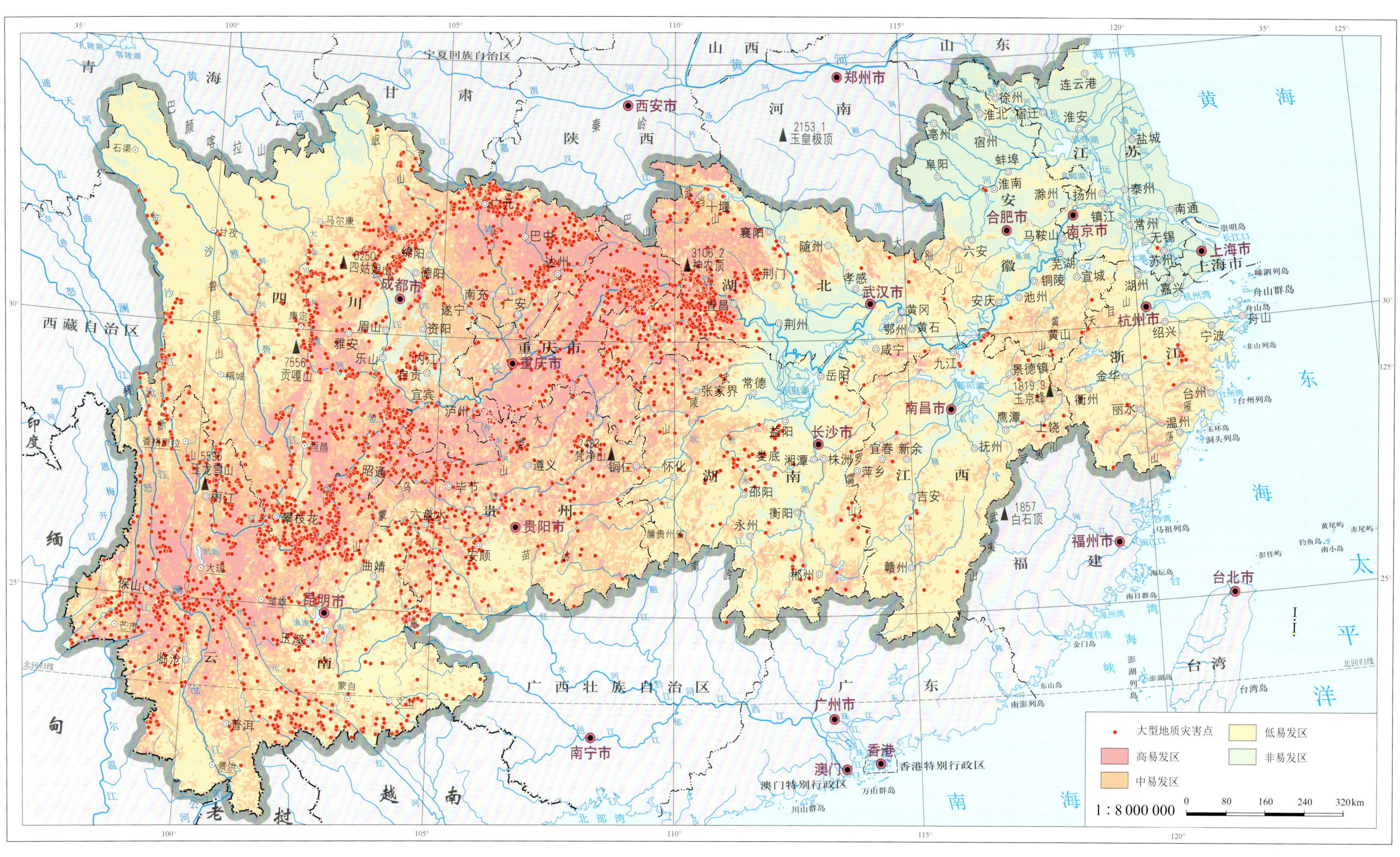

附图6 长江经济带高速铁路、过江通道及重大地质问题图

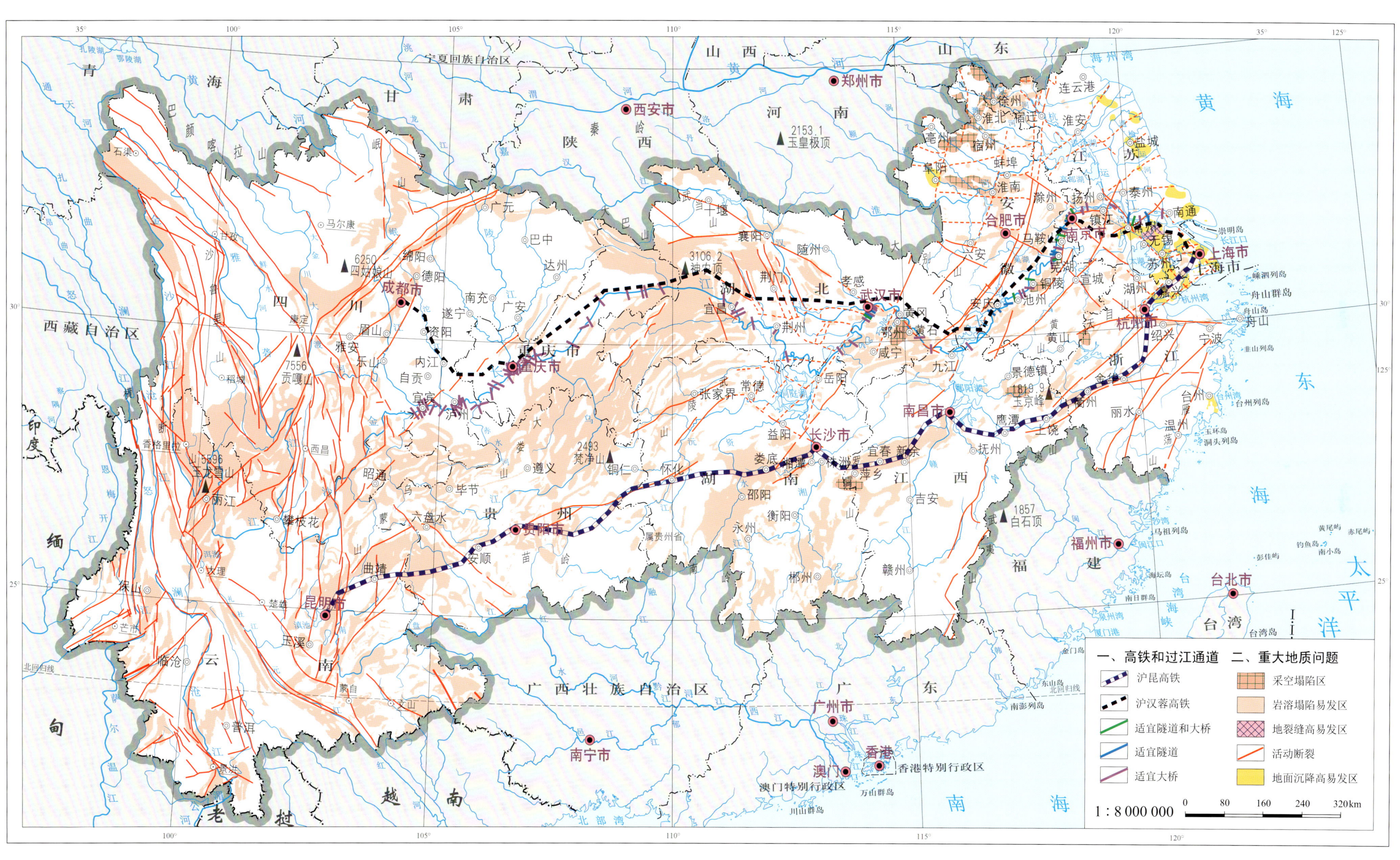

附图7 长江经济带城市群及主要城市分布图

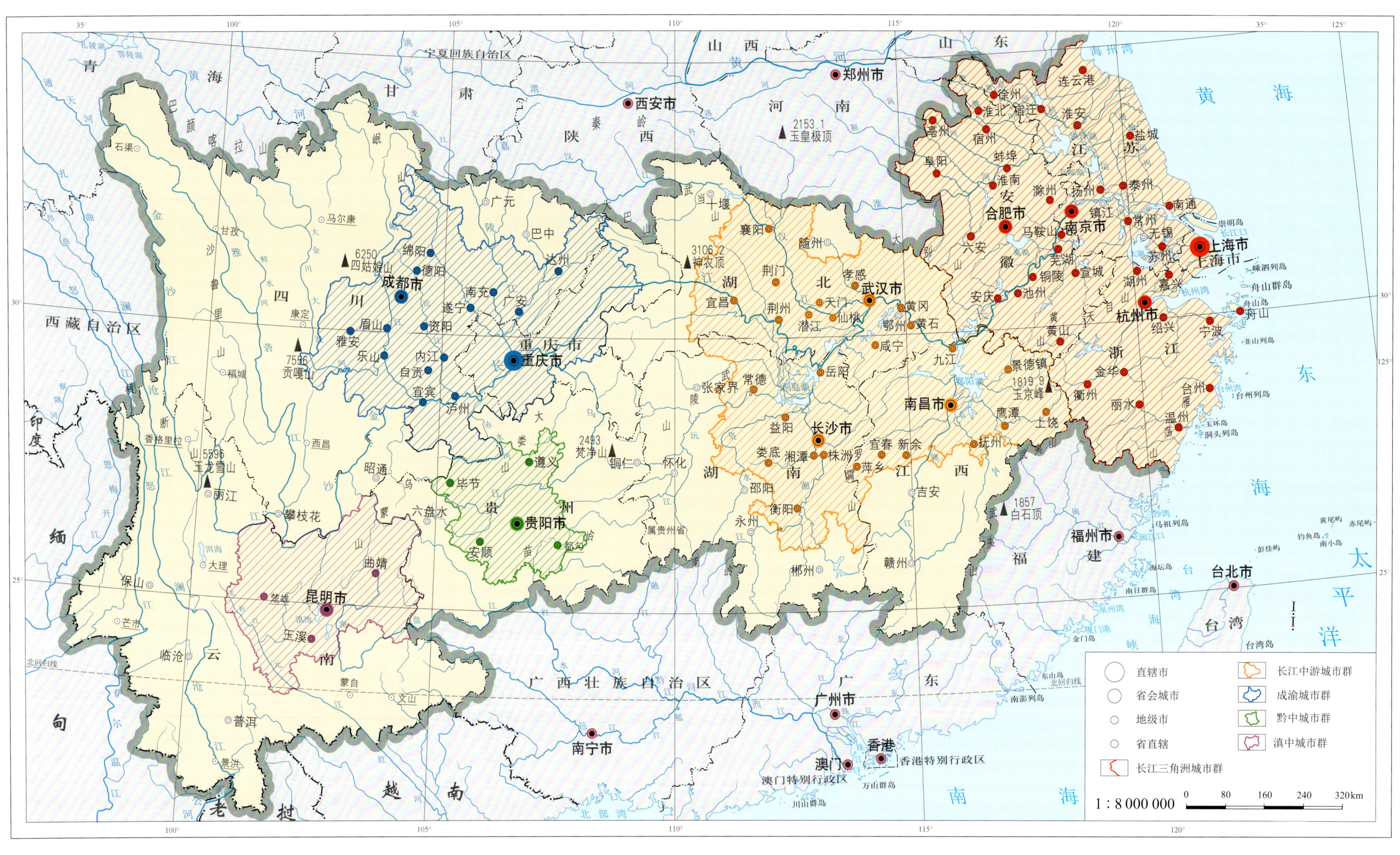

附图8 长江经济带大型矿产资源基地分布图

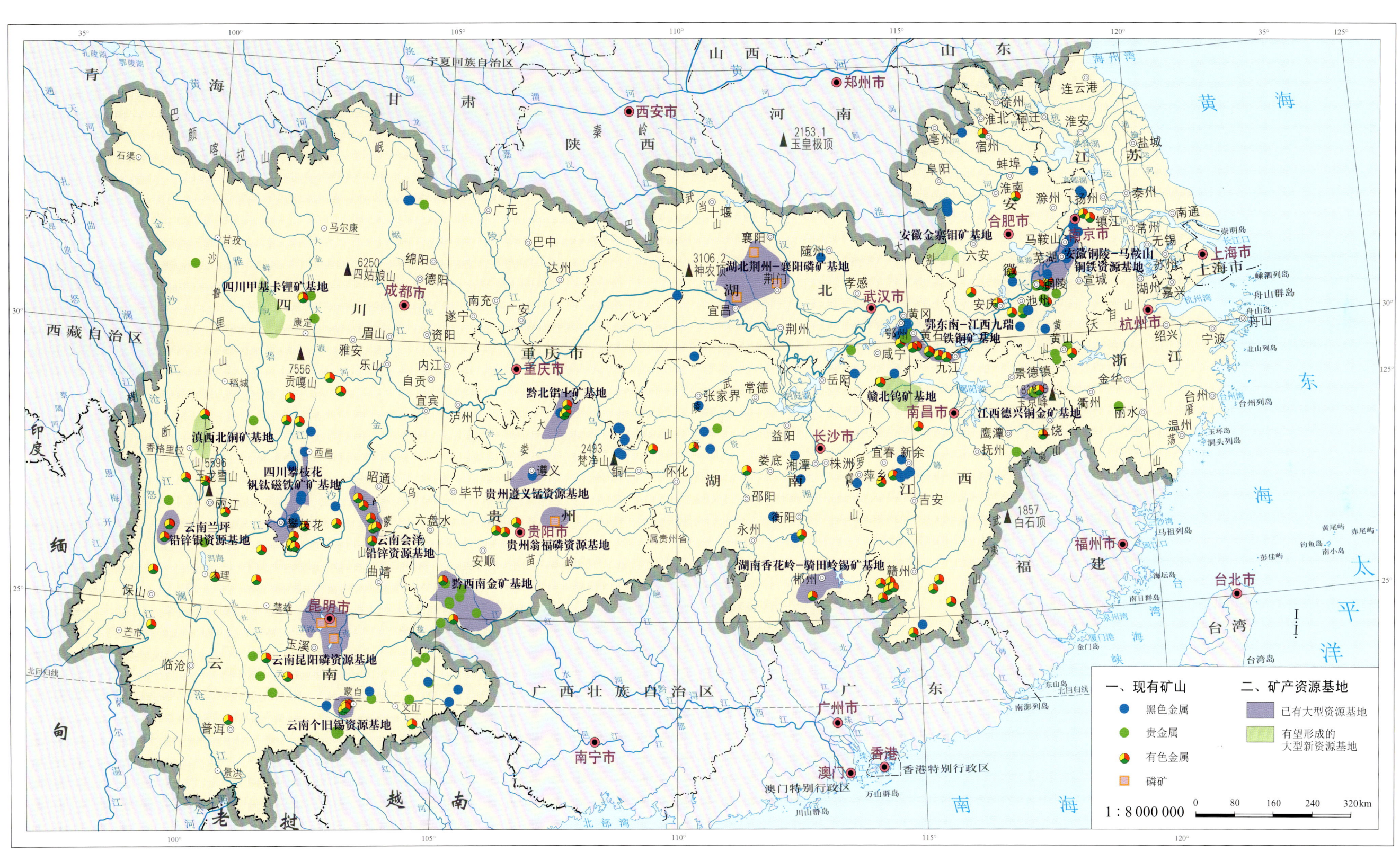

附表 1 长江经济带无重金属污染耕地和绿色富硒耕地分布

省（市）	绿色富硒耕地（万亩）	无重金属污染耕地（万亩）
上海	6	736
江苏	133	11 615
浙江	347	2 654
安徽	213	7 552
江西	325	3 339
湖北	350	7 009
湖南	256	2 240
重庆	43	2 719
四川	142	7 027
贵州	18	48
云南	3	310
合计	1836	45 249

附表 2 影响长江经济带过江通道建设的重大地质问题

所属省份	过江通道位置	重大地质问题	防控建议
江苏省	常泰	无锡-宿迁断裂	开展活动断裂详细勘查，进一步确定活动断裂位置和活动性。若活动断裂穿过规划位置，建议调整规划位置。如果不调整，则需做好工程防震减震措施和运营期地震监测
江苏省	五峰山	无锡-宿迁断裂、茅山断裂	
江苏省	张靖	金坛-南渡断裂	
江苏省	上元门	南京-湖熟断裂	
湖北省	武穴	襄广断裂、郯庐断裂	
湖北省	棋盘洲	襄广断裂	
湖北省	鄂黄第二	襄广断裂	
四川省	绵遂内宜铁路	华蓥山断裂	
四川省	白塔山	华蓥山断裂	
湖北省	武汉地铁 11 号线	岩溶塌陷	加强隐伏岩溶区岩溶地质详细勘查，查明溶洞准确位置。若规划位置存在大型溶洞，则建议调整大桥位置。如果不调整，则建议做好工程处理，并开展岩溶塌陷变形监测
湖北省	嘉鱼	岩溶塌陷	
湖北省	赤壁	岩溶塌陷	

附表 3 长江经济带过江通道方式建议

过江通道位置	比选依据	数量（条）	过江方式建议
湖北红花套、伍家岗、宜昌轨道、陡山沱；重庆安张铁路、奉节、安坪、故陵、万州绕城高速、西沱、顺溪、兴义、长寿第三、长寿第二、珞碛、雷家坡、果园、郭家沱、铁路东南环线、新田、新田港铁路、黄桷坪、鹅公岩、李家沱、小南海、韩家沱、黄桷沱、白居寺、五举沱、油溪、白沙；四川榕山、合江新城、合江县城、泰安第二、沙茜、蓝田、纳溪、安富第二、安富第一、江安第二、南溪、罗龙、盐坪坝、绵遂内宜铁路、白塔山、普和金沙江、豆坝	位于长江上游，河床深切、卵砾石层厚，不利于隧道施工，同时基岩埋藏浅，江岸稳定，有利于大桥建设	48	大桥
江苏锡通、江阴第二、五峰山、宁仪、七乡河、上元门、安徽慈湖、姑孰、弋矶山第二、龙窝湖、横港、梅龙、江口、海口、赣皖宿松、湖北武穴、棋盘洲、鄂黄第二、武汉地铁 10 号线、青山、杨泗港、沌口、嘉鱼、赤壁、石首、荆州第二、枝江	位于长江中下游，河床深切，岩土体性质不均一，河床沉积厚度小，不利于隧道施工。同时最大深水线居中，河道顺直，江面和滩地窄，有利于大桥建设	27	大桥
江苏张靖、常泰、南京地铁 4 号线、南京第五、锦文路、安徽泰山路、九华路、池安、安庆、武汉地铁 7 号线、8 号线、11 号线	位于长江中下游，最大深水线靠岸，岸线侵蚀强烈，不利于大桥建设。同时河道切割浅，岩土体性质均一，河床沉积厚度大，有利于隧道施工	12	隧道
江苏江阴第三、南京和燕路、汉中西路；安徽马鞍山、湖北路、龙山路、芜湖城南、铜陵开发区、池州	位于长江中下游，地质条件均有利于隧道和桥梁建设	8	桥梁或隧道

附表 4 长三角城市群地面沉降及其影响城市

地区	累计沉降量大于 200mm 面积（km²）	影响城市	累计最大沉降量（mm）	平均沉降速率（mm/a）
上海市	1 068.6	市区，闵行、浦东、嘉定、宝山、青浦和松江局部	2 980	5.2
苏锡常	5 240.2	苏州、吴江、昆山、太仓、常熟、张家港、无锡、江阴、常州	2 800	4.4
杭嘉湖	3 545.7	嘉兴、海宁、平湖、桐乡、嘉善、海盐、湖州东、杭州北	1 097	6.9
江苏沿海	10 590.0	盐城、大丰、阜宁、射阳、滨海、灌南、响水、南通	717	25.6

附表 5 长江中游城市群岩溶塌陷及其影响城市

岩溶塌陷地区	面积（km²）	影响城市
武汉市、黄石—鄂州、咸宁—嘉鱼	2 027	武汉、鄂州、黄石、大冶、咸宁、嘉鱼、赤壁、崇阳
瑞昌—九江—彭泽沿江地区	440	瑞昌市、九江市、湖口县、彭泽县
萍乡—丰城—乐平一带	1 630	芦溪、宜春、分宜、新余、上高、高安、樟树、丰城、乐平、弋阳
湖南长株潭地区	320	长沙岳麓、宁乡、湘潭、株洲
常德地区	229	常德
京山—钟祥地区	55.3	京山、钟祥

附表 6 成渝城市群主要地质问题及其影响城市

地级以上市	县（市、区）	地质问题
成都市	都江堰市、彭州	地震
德阳市	绵竹县、什邡	地震
绵阳市	平武县、安县	地震
雅安市	雨城区、名山区、荥经、汉源、石棉、天全、芦山、宝兴	地震及其他地质灾害
南充市	南部县、仪陇县	地质灾害
乐山市	金口河区、峨边县、马边县	地震及其他地质灾害
泸州市	叙永县、古蔺县	地质灾害
内江市	内江市	地质灾害
内江市	隆昌县	地震
宜宾市	翠屏区、筠连县、珙县、兴文县、屏山县	地质灾害
宜宾市	长宁县、高县、筠连县	地震
自贡市	自贡市	地质灾害
自贡市	自贡市、荣县、富顺	地震
重庆市	忠县、万州、云阳、涪陵	地质灾害

附表 7 长江经济带大型矿产资源基地

资源基地名称	保有资源储量	矿山总数（个）
安徽铜陵－马鞍山铜铁资源基地	铜：96.4×10⁴t 铁：6.7×10⁸t	90
鄂东南－江西九瑞铁铜矿基地	铜：331.4×10⁴t 铁：2.6×10⁸t	90
湖北荆州－襄阳磷矿基地	磷：9.7×10⁸t	164
湖南香花岭－骑田岭锡矿基地	锡：5.1×10⁴t	51
江西德兴铜金矿基地	铜：552×10⁴t 金：36.2t	23
黔西南金矿基地	金：126t	69
贵州瓮福磷资源基地	磷：2.1×10⁸t	19
云南昆阳磷资源基地	磷：5.4×10⁸t	54
贵州遵义锰资源基地	锰：2495×10⁴t	36
黔北铝土矿基地	铝土矿：4889×10⁴t	16
云南会泽铅锌资源基地	锌矿：46.8×10⁴t	9
四川攀枝花钒钛磁铁矿基地	铁：19.9×10⁸t	159
云南个旧锡资源基地	锡：27.5×10⁴t	11
云南兰坪铅锌银资源基地	铅矿：46.8×10⁴t 锌矿：640×10⁴t	17

English Version

Ⅰ. Momentous Geological Problems Needing Attention for Urban and Infrastructural Planning

1.1 The Geological Suitability Map for Planning and Development of Urban and Important Infrastructure

Regarding the factor of geological safety, the suitability of land utilization for urban and important infrastructure development in the Yangtze River Economic Zone can be divided into four levels: Ⅰ. Unsuitable area, including seismically active regions (>magnitude 5), two sides of major active faults and mined-out subsidence area; Ⅱ. Low suitable area, including high susceptibleregions with collapse, landslide, debris flow, karst collapse and ground fissure, and other marginal areas of active faults excluding those in unsuitable area; Ⅲ. The area in need of prevention and control, where the collapse, landslide and debris flow are medium-prone to happen and ground subsidence resulted from human activities are high-prone to occur; Ⅳ. Suitable area,which is the remaining part from the above-mentioned three areas and has not yet found any vital geological problems.

1.2 The Suitability Zoning Map for Port Construction along the Yangtze River (Jiangsu Segment)

According to overall assessment on the construction suitability of port and wharf along different sections of the River, the riverbanks can be graded into Level-Ⅰ, Level-Ⅱ and Level-Ⅲ. Among which, Level-Ⅰ section is very suitable for the construction of port and wharf, Level-Ⅱ section has medium suitability and Level-Ⅲ section has low suitability. The assessments indicate there are 27 Level-Ⅰ, 24 Level-Ⅱ and 35 Level-Ⅲ sections respectively. All of the Level-Ⅰ section belongs to deepwater coastline with favorable engineering geological conditions; both their channel width and accessibility can meet demand on building over 10,000dwt berth, and can be top priority for planning and preferentially developed objectives as port and wharf.

1.3 The Distribution Map of Urbanization Area in the Yangtze River Economic Zone

The principal urbanization areas in the Yangtze River Economic Zone enclose different scales of cities and towns, specifically including four types: ①metropolis with total population in excess of 5 million, namely, Shanghai, Hangzhou, Nanjing, Wuhan, Chengdu and Chongqing and other core cities in the key metropolitan coordinating regions along the Yangtze River;②large city with total population between 1 million to 5 million, including Suzhou, Changsha, Guiyang, Wenzhou, Kunming and other center cities in the provinces within the economic zone;③middle city with population between 0.5 million to 1 million, such as Taizhou, Yichang, Xiaogan, Changde, Zunyi, Ningbo, Mianyang, Shaoyang and other important cities in each province; ④small city with total population less than 0.5 million.

1.4 The Development Intensity Map of the Country's Lands in the Yangtze River Economic Zone

The development intensity of the country's lands across the zone is mainly calculated according to the proportion of the land surface for construction of urban, industrial and mining areas occupied in single grid (1km×1km). The development degree can be classified in turn from sparse to intensive as 0–20%, 20%–40%, 40%–60%, 60%–80%, 80%–100%. As a whole, the map shows a tendency of low development intensity in the west but high in the east. The highest intensive value occurs in the Yangtze River Delta Zone. The intensity index is concordant with the urban construction. The development areas encircling the major cities of every province are distributed along the Yangtze River Economic Zone.

1.5 The Distribution Map of Geohazards and Susceptablility Degree in the Yangtze River Economic Zone

The susceptible areas of landslide, collapse and debris flow are mainly distributed in the conflux area of Nujiang River, Lancang River and Jinsha River, Longmenshan Fault Zone and moderate mountainous region in Hubei, Guizhou and Yunnan provinces. There are 106,760 spots of geohazard and hidden troubles of landslide, collapse and debris flow which have been defined by investigation.

The susceptible areas of ground subsidence and ground fissures are mainly located in Shanghai, Jiangsu province, Hangzhou-Jiaxing-Huzhou area, etc. The highly susceptible area covers an area of 6,690.9km^2 and the biggest cumulative subsidence volume in central subsidence area reaches 2.63m^2. As so far, there are over 20 spots of ground fissures.

The susceptible areas of ground collapse are mainly distributed in eastern Chongqing, western Wuhan, northern Guizhou, northeastern Yunnan, middle Hunan and Xuzhou-Huaihe River Economic Zone in Anhui and Jiangsu provinces. There are 5,323 spots of ground collapse have been defined by investigation. The highly susceptible area is 23.5×10^{4}km^2.

1.6 The Distribution Map of Karst Collapses and Hazard Assessment in the Yangtze River Economic Zone

The distribution of karst collapses: there are 805 spots of karst collapse in the whole zone, consisting of soil layers collapse and 1 bedrock collapse. Apart from Shanghai, the geohazard happened in each province and municipality of the region, which specifically developed intensively in Yunnan, Guizhou, Hunan, Anhui and Jiangxi. In terms of the causes of collapse, 608 cases were triggered by human engineering activities while 154 developed under natural conditions. The human engineering activities such as mining water-discharge, groundwater mining and traffic engineering construction are the majorly contribution to the karst collapse.

The distribution of hazard assessment on karst collapses: the highly dangerous area of hazard occupies an area of about 23.5×10^{4}km^2, while the moderately dangerous area occupies an area of 11.1×10^{4}km^2, most of which are distributed in Guizhou, Yunnan, Hubei, Hunan provinces and Chongqing municipality.

1.7 The Map of Active Fault Zones and Assessment on Regional Crustal Stability in the Yangtze River Economic Zone

The distribution of active fault zones: over 150,000 years, the developed active fault zones include Dongmengou Fault, Huya Fault, Dengke-Ganzi Fault, Ganzi-Luhuo Fault, Maowen-Tianquan Fault, Longmenshan Fault, Batang Fault, Jianchuan-Sanjiangkou Fault, Lijiang-Ninglang Fault, Anninghe Fault, Macheng-Tuanfeng Fault, Maoshan Fault, Ruijin-Huichang Fault, Tanlu Fault and so on.

The characteristics of zoning for regional crustal stability: stable regions account for 32.6%, roughly stable regions 36.6%, sub-unstable regions 28.2% and unstable regions 2.6%. The former two regions are mainly distributed in mid-eastern Yangtze River Economic Zone; and most of the unstable regions include Meishan city-Jinyang county-Kunming city area, Lijiang city-Jianchuan county area and Ganluo county-Yanjin county area.

1.8 The Situation Map of Ground Subsidence and Ground Fissures in the Yangtze River Economic Zone

The regions with cumulative subsidence volume above 200mm in Suzhou-Wuxi-Changzhou area of Jiangsu province, Hangzhou-Jiaxing- Huzhou area of Zhejiang province and Shanghai municipality have reached 1/3 with a total area over 10, 000km^2. The delineation shows a tendency of connection among the above-mentioned three regions.The total surface of the coastal plain region with cumulative subsidence volume above 200mm in Yancheng and Lianyungang of Jiangsu province has reached 9,300km^2. This type of geohazard has directly and indirectly caused 362.91 billion yuan of economic loss.

II. Energy and Resources Potentiality Needing Consideration for Planning and Layout of Industrial Development

2.1 The Distribution Map of Energy Mineral Resources in the Yangtze River Economic Zone

Energy mineral resources refer to petroleum, natural gas, shale gas, coal and so on. In this region, 93 oil fields and 97 gas fields have been discovered and most of them are distributed in Sichuan Basin, Jianghan Basin and Northern Jiangsu Basin. Shale gas exploration made break-through in Fuling, Sichuan province. By the end of the year of 2013, proved recoverable reserves of petroleum is 1.41×10^8t and natural gas is 18,719.87m^3. Cumulative production of petroleum reaches on 8.6×10^8t and natural gas is $4,292.94\times10^8$m^3. By the end of the year of 2014, cumulative proved recoverable geological reserve of shale gas is $1,067.5\times10^8$m^3 and cumulative production is 15×10^8m^3. By the end of 2012, 432 coal deposits (28 ultra-large deposits and 141 large deposits) had been ascertained and almost half of deposits are producing. Till November of 2014, the cumulative coal reserves reached $1,463.09\times10^8$t with $1,037\times10^8$t of maintain reserves.

2.2 The Distribution Map of Geothermal Resources in the Yangtze River Economic Zone

The distribution characteristics of geothermal resources in the Yangtze River Economic Zone: the conductive type of geothermal fields in sedimentary basin are mainly distributed in Northern Jiangsu Basin, Jianghan Basin and Sichuan Basin; the fault type of geothermal fields in uplift mountains are mainly distributed as high-moderate temperature geothermal reserves in uplift bedding-slide plateaus and fault-uplift hilly areas of western Yunnan province; the convective type of geothermal fields mainly occurred in western Sichuan province, eastern Yunnan province and China's southeast coastal area. The average temperature is 40-45℃ at the depth of 1,000m underground, 60-80℃ at the depth of 2,000m and 90-110℃ at the depth of 3,000m. The geothermal resources in the Yangtze River Economic Zone have great exploitation potentiality with $16.090,37\times10^8$ m^3/a estimated recoverable geothermal water resources.

2.3 The Exploitation Map of Mineral Resources in the Yangtze River Economic Zone

As the core supplying region of important resources in China, the regional mineral resources are well exploited but the scale and integration of exploition are not outstanding in general. Currently there are 480 million mines and most of them have became important large bases of mining industry, including Dexing copper-gold resource base in Jiangxi, tungsten resource base in South Jiangxi, Panzhihua vanadium titanomagnetite resource base in Sichuan, gold resource base in Southwest Guizhou, Zunyi manganese resource base in Guizhou, Kunyang phosphate resource base in Yunnan, Lanping lead-zinc-silver resource base, Huize lead-zinc resource base and Gejiu tin resource base in Yunnan, etc. In 2013, the total output value of mining industry is 496.08 billion yuan with over 3 million of relevant employees and 99 developing resources-type cities. Nonetheless, the approaches of traditional resources exploitation also bring ecological environmental problems and urge green transformation.

2.4 The Distribution Map of Mineral Resources Potentiality in the Yangtze River Economic Zone

The Yangtze River Economic Zone possesses favorable exploration potentiality of mineral resources. Till date, 7 potential areas have been prospected and established, i.e. Nanjing in Jiangsu province, Wuhu and Tongling in Anhui province, Dexing and Jiujiang in Jiangxi province, Jinzhou–Xiangyang in Hubei, Panzhihua in Sichuan province, Anshun in Guizhou province, Huize in Yunnan province. The total surface of the 7 potential areas is 1.46×10^4 km^2 and the principal types of mineral resources include iron, copper, lead, zinc, gold, phosphorusand bauxite. There are 4 newly targeted potential areas distributed in Jinzhai in Anhui province, Nanchang in Jiangxi province, Ya'an in Sichuan province, Lijiang in Yunnan province, where a total area of 3,400km^2 and principal mineral types including copper, tungsten, molybdenum and lithium. Presently 9 more mineral resources potential areas can be developed and exploited, mostly are distributed in Wuzhou in Jiangxi province, Suichang-Longyou in Zhejiang province, western Hunan province and southwestern Yunnan province, with a total area of 0.96×10^4 km^2, and dominant mineral types such as lead, zinc, copper, titanium, and tin.

2.5 The Distribution Map of Metal Mineral Resources in the Yangtze River Economic Zone

The zone has rich metal mineral resources, and its available reserves for 30 kinds of minerals account for more than 50% of national total, among which tungsten, antimony and ion-type rare earth occupy predominant reserves in the world. By the end of 2012, there are 1,439 medium scale mines found (including 93 ultra large ores)105.42×10^8t of large-ultra large scale of iron ore resource and $23,713.4\times10^4$t of manganese ore resources. With respect to the production of nonferrous metal minerals by the end of 2013, China has $3,366.45\times10^4$t of proved reserves of large-ultra large copper-gold resources,4.14×10^8t of bauxite, $6,733.6\times10^4$t of lead and zinc, 560.5×10^4t of oxide tungsten and 436.8×10^4t oftin. It is estimated that by the end of 2013, in the category of precious metal minerals, there are 2,355.36t of proved cummulative reserves of large-ultra large gold resources, 73.3t of platinum and 6.21×10^4t of silver (associated silver in list).

2.6 The Distribution Map of Nonmetallic Minerals Resources in the Yangtze River Economic Zone

The Yangtze River Economic Zone has a wide-ranging types and abundant resources of nonmetallic minerals. The available reserve of phosphate accounts for 89%–90% of national total. Mineral resources such as fluorite and barite, taking dominant share in the world, all concentrate in this region. By the end of 2013, total recoverable reserve of large-ultra large phosphate ores has reached 123.32×10^8t and that of barite ores is $4,050.5\times10^4$t. They can be divided into following categories by function, i.e. special nonmetal minerals, agricultural fertilizer, chemical raw material, raw material for glass, ceramic and flame-proof material, raw material for cement, brick and tile, metallurgical flux and mold materials. The total number of proved medium-ultra large scale of nonmetallic mineral deposits has reached 2,104, among which the number of large-ultra large deposits is 786. The raw material resources including fluorite, phosphorite, sulfur and pyrite, glass, ceramic and cement are predominant and over 60% of nonmetallic minerals resources have been in mining opration.

2.7 The Distribution Map of Groundwater Resources in the Yangtze River Economic Zone

The total volume of groundwater resources in the Yangtze River Economic Zone is $3,497.75\times10^8$m^3/a, accounting for 37.8% of national total, among which 96.89% of groundwater resources ($3,388.97\times10^8$m^3/a) are freshwater distributed in inland. Till 2002, the total volume of recoverable groundwater resources is $1,186.08\times10^8$m^3/a, accounting for 33.9% of total. The volume of available pore water resources is 429.98×10^8m^3/a.The prohibited and restricted area for groundwater mining: over-exploitation on deep groundwater results in ground subsidence and ground fissures in the Yangtze River Economic Zone. The effective approach to control the subsidence is to prohibit and restrict the exploitation on groundwaterr esources. The mining activities for groundwater in Suzhou-Wuxi-Changzhou and Hangzhou-Jiaxing-Huzhou areas are prohibited while they are restricted in Shanghai, Nantong, Yancheng and Taizhou.

III. Land Quality and Geochemical Background Needing Concern in the Protection and Management for Cultivated Land

3.1 The Suitability Zoning Map for the Plantation of Green Agricultural Products in Plain and Hilly Areas in the Yangtze River Economic Zone

According to the 1∶250,000 scale of multi-purpose regional geochemical survey in 2 municipalities and 9 provinces including Shanghai and Jiangsu, we acquired high precision quantitative analysis data of 54 elements of surface soil, as well as data for corresponding landform types, soil types and land utilization. The total area of well suitable-suitable regions for planting green agricultural products in plain region covers $41.27 \times 10^4 km^2$, accounting for 69.30% of the investigated area, which are mainly distributed in Circum-Taihu Lake area, Lixia River Plain, the Yangtze-Huaihe River Plain, Cirum-Poyang Lake area, Jianghan Plain, Chengdu Plain and Yuxi, Yunnan province. The relatively-suitable area covers $18.28 \times 10^4 km^2$ accounting for 30.70%, which continuously distributes in Hunan and Guiyang and patchy distributes in Huangshi, Xiantao, Guiyang, Kunming, piedmont of Chengdu Basin, southern Jiangxi province, northeast Jiangxi, Tongling, Ningbo-Shaoxing Plain, Hangzhou-Jiaxing-Huzhou Plain, Chuzhou, Suzhou and Lianyungang, etc.

3.2 The Integrated Zoning Map of Beneficial Elements in Soil in Plain and Hilly Areas in the Yangtze River Economic Zone

According to the 1:250,000 scale of multi-purpose regional geochemical survey in 2 municipalities and 9 provinces including Shanghai and Jiangsu, we acquired high precision quantitative analysis data for 21 elements of surface soil, including N, C, P, K, S, Ca, Mg, Cl, B, Fe, Si, Mn, Mo, V, Zn, Cu, Co, I, F, Se and pH, as well as data for corresponding landform types, soil types and land utilization. The total area of the region with appropriate amount of beneficial elements covers $34.43 \times 10^4 km^2$, accounting for 54.87% of regional total, and mostly are distributed in Aba Prefecture of Sichuan province, Chengdu Basin, Circum-Dongting Lake, Circum-Poyang Lake, Anhui segment area of the Yangtze River, coastal area along northern Jiangsu, Hangzhou-Jiaxing-Huzhou plain; The total area of the region with relatively-deficient beneficial elements covers $13.88 \times 10^4 km^2$, accounting for 22.12%, and are distributed in southern Jiangxi province, the Yangtze-Huaihe River Plain, northeast Hubei province and Yuxi, Yunnan province, etc.

3.3 The Map of Soil Types in the Yangtze River Economic Zone

There are 22 types of soil in the Yangtze River Economic Zone, i.e. paddy soil, red soil, purple soil, yellow soil, moisture soil, skeleton soil, calcareous soil, yellow brown soil, coastal saline soil, laterite, latored soil, torrid red soil, lime concretion black soil, volcanic ash soil, yellow cinnamon soil, cinnamon soil, cold desert soil, brown desert soil, frigid frozen soil, peat soil and acid sulphate soil. The most widely distributed types of soil are paddy soil, red soil, purple soil and yellow soil. Paddy soils are mainly distributed in Chengdu Plain, the mid-lower reaches plain of the Yangtze River, coastal plain, and some of which are also located in intermontane valley and gentle slopes area; red soils are mainly distributed in hilly country to the south bank of the Yangtze River; most of purple soil are distributed in hilly terraces of Sichuan, Chongqing and Yunnan, while yellow soils are distributed in mountain areas of Guizhou, Sichuan, Jiangxi and Zhejiang.

3.4 The Distribution Map of Cultivated Land in the Yangtze River Economic Zone

There are three types of cultivated land in the zone, including paddy field, irrigable land and dry land. Ⅰ. Paddy fields concentrate in central and eastern Hunan and Hubei provinces, central Anhui, large area of Jiangsu, and are scattered in Yunan, Guizhou and Sichuan provinces. Zhejiang and Jiangxi provinces are also dominated by paddy fields, which are the most principal cultivated land in the Yangtze River Economic Zone. Ⅱ. Dry lands are mainly distributed in central Sichuan Basin, northern portion of Hubei, Anhui and Jiangsu with a few being scattered in Yunnan and Guizhou. Ⅲ. Irrigable lands, are mostly distributed in coastal area along eastern Jiangsu province, scattering in other areas, accounting for relatively few area.

3.5 The Integrated Zoning Map of Land and Environmental Quality in Plain and Hilly Areas in the Yangtze River Economic Zone

According to the 1:250,000 scale of multi-purpose regional geochemical survey in 2 municipalities and 9 provinces including Shanghai and Jiangsu, we acquired high precision quantitative analysis data for 54 elements of surface soil, as well as data for corresponding landform types, soil types and land utilization. The general condition of land and environmental quality in the plain area of the Yangtze River Economic Zone is favorable, among which, the total area above grade-Ⅰ (moderately clean) covers $34.84 \times 10^4 km^2$, accounting for 58.51% of the investigated area. In addition, the total area of premium-grade lands is $15.40 \times 10^4 km^2$ and largely distributes in northern Jiangsu, the Yangtze-Huaihe River Plain, Jianghan Plain and Chengdu Plain. The total surface of area below grade-Ⅲ (moderately polluted) covers $6.94 \times 10^4 km^2$ and distributed in patches in northeast Jiangxi, southern Jiangxi, Changsha-Chenzhou region in Hunan.

3.6 The Geochemical Zoning Map for Land Quality in the Plain in the Yangtze River Delta Economic Zone

The general condition of land quality in the plain in the Yangtze River Economic Zone is relatively fine. The coverage area of land above the favorable level is $11.71 \times 10^4 km^2$ accounting for 86.27% of investigated area. The area of premium quality lands covers $1.59 \times 10^4 km^2$ accounting for 11.74% which are mainly distributed in Lixia River area and Jinhua Basin, while the inferior quality lands occupies a total coverage of $2534 km^2$, accounting for 1.87% and mainly displaying scattered forms in the region.

Ⅳ. Resources and Environment Status Needing Attention for Land Exploitation and Ecological Environment Conservation

4.1 The Geomorphologic Map of the Yangtze River Economic Zone

The Yangtze River Economic Zone spans across three terraces of China's geomorphology, which is featured with complicated and diverse geomorphology and relatively complete types. There are four zones separated by Guangyuan–Lijiang, Shiyan–Shaoyang and Luan–Ningbo belts from west to east. The geomorphology can be divided into seven types based on altitude and relief, i.e. ultra-high mountains, high mountains, moderate mountains, low mountains, hilly land, bench terrace and plain. In general, taking Shiyan–Shaoyang belt as the boundary, the west is dominated by mountains and the east is plain and bench terraces. In west portion, separated by Guangyuan–Lijiang belt, where the west portion is dominated by ultra-high mountains-high mountains while the east portion is middle mountains. In the east, low hills are distributed to the south of Shaoyang–Nanjing belt while plain areas coupled with bench terraces are principal landforms to its north.

4.2 The Zoning Map of Classification for National Lands Protection in the Yangtze River Economic Zone

There are four types of protection zones in the Yangtze River Economic Zone, i.e. ① Premium cultivated lands, covering Sichuan Basin, Poyang Lake Plain and Dongting Lake Plain, etc. ②Important ecological function reserve, mainly referring to the function zones for maintaining biological diversity and preserving soil-water (e.g. Three Gorges Reservoir) and Poyang Lake Wetland, etc. ③ Protection zone for water resources security, including trunk streams of the Yangtze River and main tributaries and lakes along the River. ④ Protection zone for ecological human settlements mainly focusing on the urban clusters in the Yangtze River delta, the Yangtze-Huaihe River Plain, Wuhan, Changsha-Zhuzhou-Xiangtan area, Circum-Poyang Lake area, Chengdu-Chongqing belt, central Yunnan and central Guizhou. All the above-mentioned areas are featured with highly dense population and industry, well-developed social economy and relatively heavy pressure on ecological environmental human settlements, calling for special protection.

4.3 The Zoning Map of Ecological Function in the Yangtze River Economic Zone

There are four types of important ecological function reserve in the Yangtze River Economic Zone:①The function zones for maintaining biological diversity including Sichuan-Yunnan eco-function reserve and Nanling Mountainous Region eco-function reserve for forests and biological diversity; Qinling-Bashan ecological function reserve and Wuling Mountain eco-function reserve.②The function zones for preserving soil-water consist of areas in Three Gorges Reservoir, Dabie Mountainous Region and Wuling Mountain.③Important wetlands comprise Norgay prairie wetland, Jinjiang wetland in the Yangtze River, middle-lower reaches wetland in Huaihe River, Poyang Lake wetland.④ Principal source regions of river and lake, including Pearl River source, Dongting Lake source region, Huaihe River source and Ganjiang-Minjiang source.

4.4 The Distribution Map of Ecological Land Utilization in the Yangtze River Economic Zone

The utilization of ecological land in the zone can be divided into six types. The first and the principal type is forest, which shows concentrated distribution apart from that in Anhui, northern Jiangsu and Sichuan Basin. The second is meadows concentrated in western Sichuan nearby relative high altitude area of Qinghai-Tibet Plateau. The third is plantation scattering irregularly in each province and regions. The fourth is water surface, mostly being distributed in the middle-lower reaches of the Yangtze River, as well as some rivers and lakes in its upper reaches. The fifth is mudflats and swamps, among which the inland mudflats are distributed in reaches area around rivers and lakes, coastal mudflats in continental coastline, swamps in upper-middle reaches of the Yangtze River. The sixth is glacier and firn line zone, which is a rare type of land utilization and distributed in high altitude area in the upper reaches of the River.

4.5 The Distribution Map of Ecologically Sensitive Regions in the Yangtze River Economic Zone

There are 1,076 natural reserves in the Yangtze River Economic Zone, among which 123 spots are state-level, 264 spots are provincial-level, occupying an area of $6.5\times10^4 km^2$ and $5.8\times10^4 km^2$ respectively. The proportion of reserves in each province ranges from 1.53% to 18.54%, including the biggest proportion in Sichuan province, Chongqing municipality, and the least in Jiangsu and Zhejiang provinces.There are 296 scenic areas and landscapes among which 223 spots are state-level, 783 forest parks among which 162 are state-level, 91 geoparks among which 10 are world-level.

4.6 The Recommended Map of Protection for Major Lakes and Wetlands in the Yangtze River Economic Zone

The wetlands in the region can be classified into five types, i.e. offshore and coastal wetlands distributed along coastal area of eastern China, riverine wetlands distributed along the trunk stream and tributaries, lake wetlands in middle-east portion of the economic zone, marsh in Aba and Ganzi Prefectures of Sichuan province, and constructed wetlands including major reservoirs and surrounding areas.As to wetland restoration and protection zones–based on the average water level and maximum flood level of flood season in current wetlands, if the wetlands would be restored into the scale of 1970s, the restoration is suggested to be focused in Poyang Lake, Honghu Lake, Dongting Lake, Taihu Lake, Hongze Lake and Chaohu Lake, which plan to expand the current total area of $1.103,1\times10^4 km^2$ into $1.4\times10^4 km^2$ with 30% of increased range.

4.7 The Groundwater Pollution Status Map of the Plain Area in the Yangtze River Delta Economic Zone

In the samples extracted from the shallow groundwater, the heavy polluted samples account for 25.19% of the total samples, moderately polluted samples account for 20.19%, while mildly polluted samples 36.74% and unpolluted samples 35%. In deep groundwater, the heavy polluted samples account for 16%, moderately polluted samples account for 16%, while mildly polluted samples 35% and unpolluted samples 33%. The groundwater pollution was majorly attributed to disorderly discharge of the industrial wastes and overuse of fertilizers.

4.8 The Trizone Polymers Pollution Map of the Groundwater in the Plain Area of the Yangtze River Delta Economic Zone

The evaluation results for trizone polymers pollution in shallow groundwater indicate that the heavy polluted samples account for 21.50% and are distributed in the whole economic zone, concentrated in northern flank of the Yangtze River Delta, the southern flank of the estuary of the Yangtze River and northern part of Hangzhou Bay, which is most extensive in agricultural region of the well-developed area.

4.9 The Pollution Map of Heavy Metals and Organic Components in the Plain Area of the Yangtze River Delta Economic Zone

The evaluation results for the pollution of heavy metals and organic components in the shallow groundwater indicate that the heavy polluted samples account for 5.18%, relatively concentrating along the River, the estuary of the River, and the conjunct area between Shanghai, Kunshan and Jiaxing. While this evaluation in deep groundwater shows that heavy polluted samples account for 3.74% and are majorly distributed along the River segment of Yangzhou and Taizhou, and a few in central regions of counties in Nantong.

4.10 The Suitability Zoning Map of Geological Storage for CO_2 in the Yangtze River Economic Zone

The total surface of sedimentary basins in the Yangtze River Economic Zone is about $65.1\times10^4 km^2$. The whole potentiality for geological storage of CO_2 reaches $902.89\times10^8 t$, among which the storage capacity of deep saline aquifer contains $823.14\times10^8 t$ of storage capacity, accounting for 91%; the oil field is $5.68\times10^8 t$, accounting for 1%; and the gas field is $74.07\times10^8 t$, accounting for 8%. The suitability appraisal indicates that the area of suitable–moderately suitable storage is about $15.6\times10^4 km^2$, accounting for 24% of total appraisal area with about $384\times10^8 t$ of storage capacity which accounts for 42.5% of total capacity; mildly suitable area is $37.2\times10^4 km^2$, accounting for 57.1% with $495.3\times10^8 t$ of storage capacity accounting for 54.9%; the relatively unsuitable–unsuitable area is $12.3\times10^4 km^2$, accounting for 18.9% of the whole appraisal area.

Ⅴ. National Land Resources and Environmental Status in Coastal Area along the Yangtze River Delta

5.1 The Back-up Resources Map of Tidal Flat Areas in the Yangtze River Delta Economic Zone

The potential areas to develop the back-up resources of tidal flat in the region can be divided into three types: the first type is distributed above the average high-water line with a total area of $460 km^2$; the second type is distributed in the intertidal zone between coastal line and maximum average low water line, which is generally exposed during the period of maximum low water with an area of $3,024 km^2$; the third type is distributed between the low water line and the neritic sea area within its 5m depth where the surface cannot be exposed naturally and the total area is $2,080 km^2$.

5.2 The Distribution Map of Mineral Resources in Sea Area of the Yangtze River Delta Economic Zone

The data shows that the southern Yellow Sea Basin has $2.98\times10^8 t$ of petroleum resources and $1,847\times10^8 m^3$ of natural gas; the shelf basin in East China Sea has $7.2\times10^8 t$ of petroleum and $36,000\times10^8 m^3$ of natural gas. Solid mineral resources are dominated by marine sand and littoral placer deposits, among which, the sea area of Zhoushan has a large potentiality of marine sand deposits with an exploration reserves of $6,150\times10^4 t$.

5.3 The Distribution Map of Coastal Wetlands in the Yangtze River Delta Economic Zone

This region embraces plentiful coastal wetlands resources with a total area of $1.323\times10^4 km^2$. The Yancheng in Jiangsu province, known as "the Capital of Oriental Wetlands", is the biggest coastal wetland in Asian continental margin, which is listed as the world key protection zones for wetlands. The development and construction along the coast and tideland reclamation have severely threatened the coastal wetlands, resulting in pollution aggravation, alien species invasion and tidal flat siltation.

5.4 The Bathyorographical Map of Sea Area in the Yangtze River Delta Economic Zone

The Yangtze River Delta is one of biggest estuary deltas in the world, and its tidal sand ridges in North Jiangsu and East China Sea shelf are one of largest tidal deposition systems. The subaqueous relief is generally gentle except the area around Zhoushan islands with dramatic changes. Jiangsu radial sandy ridges cluster is constituted by over 10 radial sand ridges extending ten to one hundred of kilometers, and the nearshore portion of most of these ridges would emerge during the low tide.

APPENDIX

Geological Survey in Support of the Yangtze River Economic Zone(2015)
—Four Favorable Resource Environmental Conditions and Four Momentous Geological Problems in the Yangtze River Economic Zone

In support of the development strategy of the Yangtze River Economic Zone (YEZ), China Geological Survey, MLR, together with the land and resources departments of the 11 provinces (municipalities) within the YEZ, made a systematic collation of previous geological survey achievements and a research on the resource and environment conditions and momentous geological problems in this zone. Initial research results indicate that the YEZ has superior arable land, shale gas, geothermal and lithium resources, including $4.5×10^8$mu heavy metal-free arable land(1mu=666.67m^2), three national-level shale gas Exploration and Development(E&D) bases with proved reserve of $5,441×10^8$m^3, annual available geothermal energy equivalent to $2.4×10^8$t standard coal or 19% of the coal consumption of 2014, and the largest energy metal-lithium deposit in Asia. Its resource and environment conditions are conducive to the development of modern agriculture, clean energy and strategic new industries. Nevertheless, the active faults, karst collapse, surface subsidence, and other momentous geological problems in the YEZ have contributed negatively to the planning and construction of river-crossing channels, high-speed railways and urban agglomerations. There are 12 river-crossing channels with many geological hazard threats to the 19% lines of Hukun High-speed Railway. Besides, attention must also be paid to the arable land soil acidification, groundwater pollution and mine environmental geological problems that are prominent and preventing the construction of the green ecological corridor.

6.1 Four favorable resource environmental conditions supporting the YEZ

The YEZ has abundant heavy metal-free arable land resources, good potential for exploiting shale gas, geothermal energy and other clean energy, and large reserves of strategic mineral resources such as lithium, rare earth, vanadium-titanium and tungsten-stannum, which is good for supporting the development of the YEZ.

(1)The $4.5×10^8$mu of heavy metal-free arable land and $1,836×10^4$mu of green Se-rich arable land provide good conditions for developing modern agriculture and characteristic agriculture

The YEZ owns $6.8×10^8$mu arable land, accounting for 33.4% of China's total arable land area. According to a geochemical survey on the quality of the $5.4×10^8$mu arable land, the environmental quality of the arable land is generally good, with heavy metal-free arable land totalling $4.5×10^8$mu (Table 1), accounting for 83.3% of the surveyed area and mainly distributed in the Sichuan Basin, Jianghan Plain, Poyanghu Plain, Caohu Plain, Dongtinghu Plain and Taihu Plain. The heavy metal-free arable land is to be first included as permanent basic farmland where food production core areas and main farm produce preponderant areas will be created.

The survey discovered $1,836×10^4$mu green Se-rich arable land (Table 1 and Figure 1) mainly located in the Chengdu Plain, Jianghan Plain, Poyanghu Plain, Taihu Plain and Jinqu Basin, with Hunan, Hubei, Jiangxi, Anhui and Zhejiang province each possessing more than $200×10^4$mu Se-rich arable land. It is recommendable to promote the experience of Fengcheng,Jiangxi and Enshi, Hubei in developing Se-rich arable land, properly plan and utilize the Se-rich arable land resources, and create a number of Se-rich industry parks or famous, characteristic, high-quality farm produce industry bases.

(2)The $15.5×10^{12}$m^3 of recoverable shale gas, accounting for 62% of the nation's total shale gas, provides good conditions for building a clean, low-carbon energy industry zone

The YEZ has tremendous potential for shale gas resources, boasting $15.5×10^{12}$m^3 of recoverable resource which is 62% of the nation's total recoverable resource. So far, China has a proved geological reserve of $5,441×10^8$m^3 of shale gas, concentrated in Fuling of Chongqing, Changning–Weiyuan of Sichuan and Zhaotong of Yunnan of the YEZ, among which Fuling has a proved geological reserve of $3,806×10^8$m^3 of shale gas and the first shale gas development base built in China with annual capacity of $35×10^8$m^3.

With the support of the Ministry of Finance, China Geological Survey, MLR has made a succession of great discoveries and progresses in shale gas survey this year. Among them are the shale gas survey in Yichang of Hubei that yielded 70m-thick hydrocarbon-bearing rock formation, indicating tremendous potential for shale gas resources; the natural gas survey in Zunyi of Guizhou reported important discoveries involving two new thick petroliferous measures, signaling satisfactory gas-bearing property of the underlying shale gas that would drive natural gas and shale gas survey in new measures of new regions across the southern part of China; and important progresses in the shale gas survey implemented in western Zigui of Hubei and western Cili of Hunan. More efforts are to be employed in shale gas resource survey and exploration by organizing the third round of public bidding for shale gas exploration blocks to involve more qualified and financially and technically strong market players into shale gas E&D, expediting the construction of the three national integrated shale gas development pilot zones including Fuling of Chongqing, accelerating technical innovation and boosting shale gas-related industries.

(3)The abundant shallow geothermal energy and hot-water geothermal resources with annual available heat equivalent to $2.4×10^8$t standard coal that are equivalent to 19% of the coal consumption in 2014, are good for boosting urban energy conservation and emissions reduction, and geothermal-related industries.

The survey and assessment indicate that the planned areas in the 11 provinces(municipalities) of the YEZ have tremendous potential for shallow geothermal energy, with annual available heat equivalent to $2×10^8$t standard coal. If this energy is substantially exploited and utilized by using geothermal pump systems, the annual cooling area in summer will be $24.6 ×10^8$m^2 and the annual heating area in winter will be $44.2×10^8$m^2, reducing $1.66×10^8$t of CO_2 emission every year. Geothermal energy utilization projects are present in all the 11 provinces(municipalities). In fact, there are 720 such projects all together, covering more than $900×10^4$m^2. The economic and social benefits are remarkable. Hot-water geothermal resources are chiefly distributed in the Sichuan Basin, Jianghan Basin, Subei Basin, Huaibei Plain and the mountainous areas of western Sichuan and western Yunnan (Figure 2), with $69.3×10^8$m^3 of recoverable geothermal water every year, equivalent to $0.4×10^8$t standard coal, of which only 1.2% is utilized every year. It would be necessary to make more efforts in nonprofit geological exploration on shallow geothermal energy and hot-water geothermal resources, reduce the risks of commercial exploration, and encourage exploitation and utilization through price subsidies, tax reliefs or other policies to support geothermal heating and cooling, greenhouse cultivation and hot spring tourism.

(4) The large reserves of strategic mineral resources such as lithium and rare earth are good for pushing forward emerging industries that include new material, high-end manufacturing and new energy automobiles, and so on

The YEZ possess more than 80% of the country's rare earth and titanium reserves, and lithium, tungsten, stannum and vanadium reserves take up more than 50% of the country's total. The largest energy metal-lithium deposit in Asia has been discovered in Jiajika of Sichuan, with a proved resource reserve of $188×10^4$t. A super molybdenum deposit has been discovered in Jinzhai of Anhui, with a resource reserve of $246×10^4$t, ranking the first in Asia and the second in the world. It has the world-leading large reserve of heavy rare earth, mainly distributed in Ganzhou, Jiangxi and Yueyang, and Hunan, etc. The proved vanadium-titanium reserve is $650×10^8$t, mainly distributed in Sichuan, Yunnan, etc. The proved tungsten-stannum reserve $650×10^4$t, mainly distributed in Jiangxi, Hunan, Yunnan. It is recommendable to make the best use of strategic mineral resources such as lithium, molybdenum, vanadium- titanium and tungsten-stannum, to boost strategic emerging industries that include lithium battery, rocket and thermonuclear reaction fuel, special alloy, superconducting material and aerospace industry, etc.

6.2 Four momentous geological problems in the YEZ

The YEZ spans across three terraces of China's geomorphology, which is featured with complicated and diverse geomorphology and relatively complete types. Geological problems such as active faults, karst collapses, landslides, rock falls, debris flows and surface subsidence occur frequently. The survey reveals 94 main active faults (Figure 3), $23.5×10^4$km^2 of high karst collapse-prone regions (Figure 4), $10.7×10^4$ landslides, rock falls and debris flows disaster hazardous points (Figure 5) and approximately $2×10^4$km^2 of serious surface subsidence regions, to which great attention will have to be paid when planning and implementing the river-crossing channels, high-speed railways and important city agglomerations.

(1)83 of the 95 planned river-crossing channels have good geological suitability while 12 have poor geological suitability. Further geological investigation would be necessary in respect of the active faults and karst collapse problems to determine the proper location and cross-river method for the channels.

According to the effects of active faults and karst collapse on the safety of the river-crossing channels, the geological suitability of the locations for the channels was preliminarily assessed. The result indicates that the locations for 83 of the 95 planned river-crossing channels have good geological suitability while 12 have poor geological suitability (Table 2 and Figure 6): the locations for nine channels, including Changtai of Jiangsu, Wuxue of Hubei and Baitashanof Sichuan, are subject to active faults, while Wuhan Line 11, Jiayu and Chibi of Hubei are exposed to karst collapse. In planning and implementing the river-crossing channels, it would be important to conduct further geological investigation and determine proper locations for the channels.

The cross-river options for the 95 channels were preliminary compared according to engineering geological suitability. As the 48 river-crossing channels in the upper reaches of the Yangtze River are located in the river sections where the watercourses are deeply cut and riverbed is thickly covered with pebble gravel, which is not good for building tunnels, while the bedrock is shallowly buried and the bank is steady, which are good for building bridges. So building a bridge across the river would be a suitable choice. In view of the cut depth of the watercourses, the thickness and homogeneity of the riverbed deposits, the deepwater horizon of the rivers and the bank stability, 27 of the river-crossing channels in the middle and lower reaches of the Yangtze River should be built in the form of a bridge, 12 in the form of a tunnel and 8 in the form of either a bridge or a tunnel (Table 3). Further investigation of the underwater topographical and hydrological conditions of the watercourses, the engineering geology of the riverbed deposits, and shoreline stability, combining with construction technology and traffic conditions, would be necessary to determine the proper cross-river method.

(2)434km of the Hukun high-speed railway line is exposed to geological hazard, for which strengthened monitoring, early warning and control would be necessary; great attention of the problems such as karst collapse and soft soil subsidence should be paid to the planned route for Nanjing–Anqing and Wuhan–Wanzhou sections of Huhanrong High-speed Railway

The 2,264km long Hukun High-speed Railway runs through the middle and lower Yangtze plains, Hunan-Jiangxi hilly–mountains and Yunnan–Guizhou Plateau. 434km of this railway line is exposed to geological hazards, and 24km of the Jiaxing section runs through surface subsidence regions. Recent years' measurements indicate that, while the overall subsidence tends to slow down, local areas' annual subsidence rate is still greater than 10mm. Hence more efforts should be made in monitoring groundwater level variation and surface subsidence. Along the Zhangshu–Pingxiang section in Jiangxi, Xiangtan–Loudi section in Hunan and Pu'an–Panxian section in Guizhou, karsts are developed and coals are concentrated. The huge volumes of groundwater drained during coal mining could induce surface subsidence anytime,it has a negative impact on the operation safety of the 392km high speed railway. It is recommendable to strengthen monitoring groundwater level and surface collapse or deformation caused by groundwater drainage in the coal mine areas along the line. Along the Songming section in Yunnan, active faults are developed. 18km of the section runs through IX ~X seismic intensity zones. Many earthquakes have taken place in history, with that in 1833 being M8. It is recommendable to take seismic mitigation measures against earthquake and perform micro-motion monitoring during operation.

When selecting the route for the Nanjing–Anqing and Wuhan–Wanzhou sections of the planned Huhanrong riverside high–speed railway, great attention should be paid to geological problems such as karst collapse and soft soil subsidence. Along the Nanjing–Anqing section, the area of karst covers 1,780km^2 in Fangcheng–Tongling–Chizhou in the south bank of the Yangtze River, where more than 100 karst collapses have already taken place. In the meantime, soft soil extends in large, continuous patches along the south bank of the Yangtze River, covering 4,900km^2. In the north bank's Hexian–Wuwei–Anqing area, on the contrary, the geological conditions are good. Hence preference should be given to the Nanjing–Wuewi–Anqing route. As to the Wuhan–Wanzhou section, the Qianjiang–Jingzhou–Zhijiang area is exposed to serious soft soil problems: the lines with soft soil thickness larger than 5m total 190km; the Tianmen–Jingmen area contains mass karst and mining subsidence regions covering 2,400km^2; while in the Tianmen–Dangyang area, the bedrock is shallowly buried and the subgrade is highly stable. Hence preference should be given to the Wuhan–Tianmen–Dangyang–Wanzhou route.

(3)The main geological problems for the Yangtze River Delta, Middle Reaches of the Yangtze River and Chengyu Urban Agglomeration are surface subsidence, karst collapse, landslide, rock fall and debris flow hazards, for which urban geological risk assessment would be necessary to ensure proper planning of the urban layout.

The Yangtze River Delta Urban Agglomeration has experienced an urban sprawl leading to serious over-exploitation of groundwater and heavy regional surface subsidence, especially Shanghai, Suzhou-Wuxi-Changzhou and Hangzhou-Jiaxing-Huzhou, where the subsidence areas with accumulated subsidence greater than 200mm total nearly 10,000km^2, though subsidence has been effectively controlled after years of efforts and the subsidence rate has slowed down: the subsidence was commonly lower than 7mm in 2014. However, new signs of surface subsidence have been discovered in Yanchengand Dafeng of Jiangsu and tend to expand. The subsidence areas with accumulated subsidence greater than 200mm total more than 10,000km^2 (Table 4), the maximum being more than 25mm in 2014. It would be necessary to regulate the groundwater exploitation in Shanghai, Suzhou-Wuxi-Changzhou and Hangzhou-Jiaxing-Huzhou where surface subsidence tends to slow down, strictly control the groundwater exploitation in the coastal areas of Jiangsu where surface subsidence is intensifying, and further strengthen the monitoring, early warning and risk control of surface subsidence.

Urbanization of the Middle reaches of Yangtze River Agglomeration is typically challenged by karst collapse risks. Survey reveals that the high susceptable regions with karst collapse are chiefly distributed in Wuhan, Huangshi–Ezhou riverside region, Ruichang–Jiujiang–Pengze riverside region, Leping–Fengcheng–Pingxiang region and Ningxiang of Hunan, where 19 urban planning zones are exposed to karst collapse, covering 4,700km^2 (Table 5). Wuhan, which is the most exposed to karst collapse, has suffered 23 karst collapses over the past 10 years, of which 17 was induced by pile foundation implementation or groundwater drainage. It is therefore important to assess the karst collapse risk zones of the urban construction land, strengthen the prevention, monitoring and early warning of karst collapse, and regulate the project implementation and construction.

Urbanization of the Chengyu Agglomeration (Figure 7) is chiefly challenged by earthquake, landslide, rockfall and debris flow risks. A number of important towns in 24 counties/cities, including Dujiangyan, Shimian and Baoxing, are situated along the Longmenshan fault belt or Yingjing-Yanjin fault belt, where they are heavily subject to earthquake. 26 cities at or above county level, including Hanyuan, Pingshan, Yunyang and Wangzhou, are situated on the periphery of the Sichuan Basin, where they are exposed to landslide, rock fall and debris flow hazard (Table 6). It would be necessary to limit the urban population of the areas subject to active faults, properly plan the construction of towns in these areas, and make more efforts in the risk assessment, monitoring, early warning and comprehensive management of geological disasters in mountainous towns in western Sichuan and northeastern Chongqing.

(4)Construction of the ecological corridor should be paid great attention to arable land acidification, groundwater pollution and mine geological environmental destruction, for which measures should be taken to limit arable land acidification, strengthen groundwater management and protection, boost the transformation and upgrading of mineral industry, and the construction of green mines.

The survey reveals 2.3×10^{8}mu acidic arable land in the YEZ, accounting for 43% of the surveyed area. The acidic arable land is mainly located in Jiangxi, Hunan, Ningbo–Taizhou coastal area and Jinhua Quzhou Basin. Compared with the result of the second national soil survey, some areas display remarkable arable land acidification trend. As acidification can activate heavy metals in the arable land, result in the leach of nutrient elements and impair the workability of the arable land, it would be necessary to control the pollutant emission of acidic substances and the application of acidic fertilizers, limit the acidification trend of arable land, implement crop rotation and cause the arable land to turn towards better quality.

The suevey reveals the underground water in YEZ has been polluted seriously by nitrogen and heavy metals, especially organics.With 17% of the pollution samples exceeding the limits,nitrogen pollutants in groundwater are primarily nitrate and ammonia-nitrogen, with 14.1% of the groundwater exceeding the permitted nitrogen limits. The main victims are the agricultural areas. The over-limit ratio of heavy metals such as mercury, cadmium and chromium is 3.5%, sporadically found on the outskirts of cities and in the vicinity of industrial or mining facilities. The over-limit ratio of toxic or hazardous organic pollutants such as carbon tetrachloride (CTC) is 0.6%, mostly scattered in or around industrial zones. It is therefore important to control groundwater pollution in and around source regions and towns, focus on prevention and natural restoration, combine monitoring and early warning with engineering treatment, and inhibit groundwater deterioration.

Of the 5.4×10^{4}mines in the YEZ, the iron, manganese, plumbum and zinc mines are mostly small-sized dispersive mining facilities. Large and medium-sized mines make up only 7%, which is lower than the country's average of 10%. Traditional exploitation and utilization methods have resulted in heavy destruction to mine geological environment. By 2014, the destructed land amounted up to approximately 5,000km^2; the stock of solid waste was 84×10^{8}t; and the annual wastewater emission was more than 27 ×10^{8}m^3. It is recommendable to expedite mining intensification and updating, strengthen the construction of the 14 large mineralresource bases (Table 7 and Figure 8); complete the construction of the 227 national-level green mine pilot zones within the shortest time, carry out green mines construction vigorously, improve the mine geological environment and maintain a balance between mines and the local areas.

6.3 Geological work scenarios of the 13th Five-Year Plan period in support of the YEZ

During period of the 13th Five-Year Plan, the Fifth Plenary Session of the 18th Central Party Committee Spirit and the Requires about development strategy of the YEZ which is put forward by "The proposal of the Cental Committee of the Communist Party of China on the 13th Five-Year Plan for the Development of National Economy and Social Development" will be carried out on an all-round way by China Geological Survey, MLR, targeting the major tasks of supporting the functional upgrading of gold waterways, building three-dimensional transport corridors, updating industries, building new urbanization and creating green ecological corridors, oriented at studying and solving the major geological problems that affect and restrict the development of the YEZ, and carrying out geological survey in the YEZ, deployed in the "four economic zones" (the Yangtze River Delta, Wanjiang, Middle Reaches of the Yangtze River and Chengyu), "three development lines" (riverside, seaside and high-speed lines) and "four key regions" (major engineering regions, important metallogenic regions, major problem regions and important ecological regions), and involving six tasks:

First, environmental geological survey on the key metallogenic regions of the Yangtze River Delta, Middle Yangtze River and Chengyu Agglomerations around the new urbanization strategy. Second, mineral resource survey on the Middle and Lower Yangtze River, Three-River(Nujing River,Langcang River,Jinsha River) Region in Southwest China, western Hunan and western Hubei, and shale gas resource survey on Sichuan-Chongqing, western Hubei and Yunnan-Guizhou around industry upgrading. Third, engineering geological survey on riverside, seaside and along high-speed railway development zones around the construction of major project and major infrastructures.Fourth, karst collapse survey and active fault survey in main fault belts along the Upper and Middle Yangtze River around momentous geological problems.Fifth, 1:250,000 geochemical survey of arable land quality in the central and western regions of China and 1:50,000 survey in eastern China around modern agriculture. And sixth, environmental geological survey on ecologic fragile regions including Danjiangkou reservoir region, Poyanghu region and Three Gorges reservoir region around the construction of ecological corridors.

In order to step up the geological survey of the YEZ, China Geological Survey, MLR will convene a meeting "Symposium on the Geological Survey of the YEZ" together with the land and resources departments of the 11 provinces (municipalities) of the YEZ, establish an innovative interlocked central-local coordination mechanism for geological work, with the support of the Ministry of Finance and following the principle of administrative and financial power division between the central and local governments, a 1.2 billion-yuan central government fund, local financial funds, would be arranged to advance geological survey, and set up a land and resources environmental carrying capacity assessment, monitoring and early warning system to provide greater support for the development strategy of the YEZ.

Figure 1 Heavy metal-free and Se-rich arable land in the YEZ

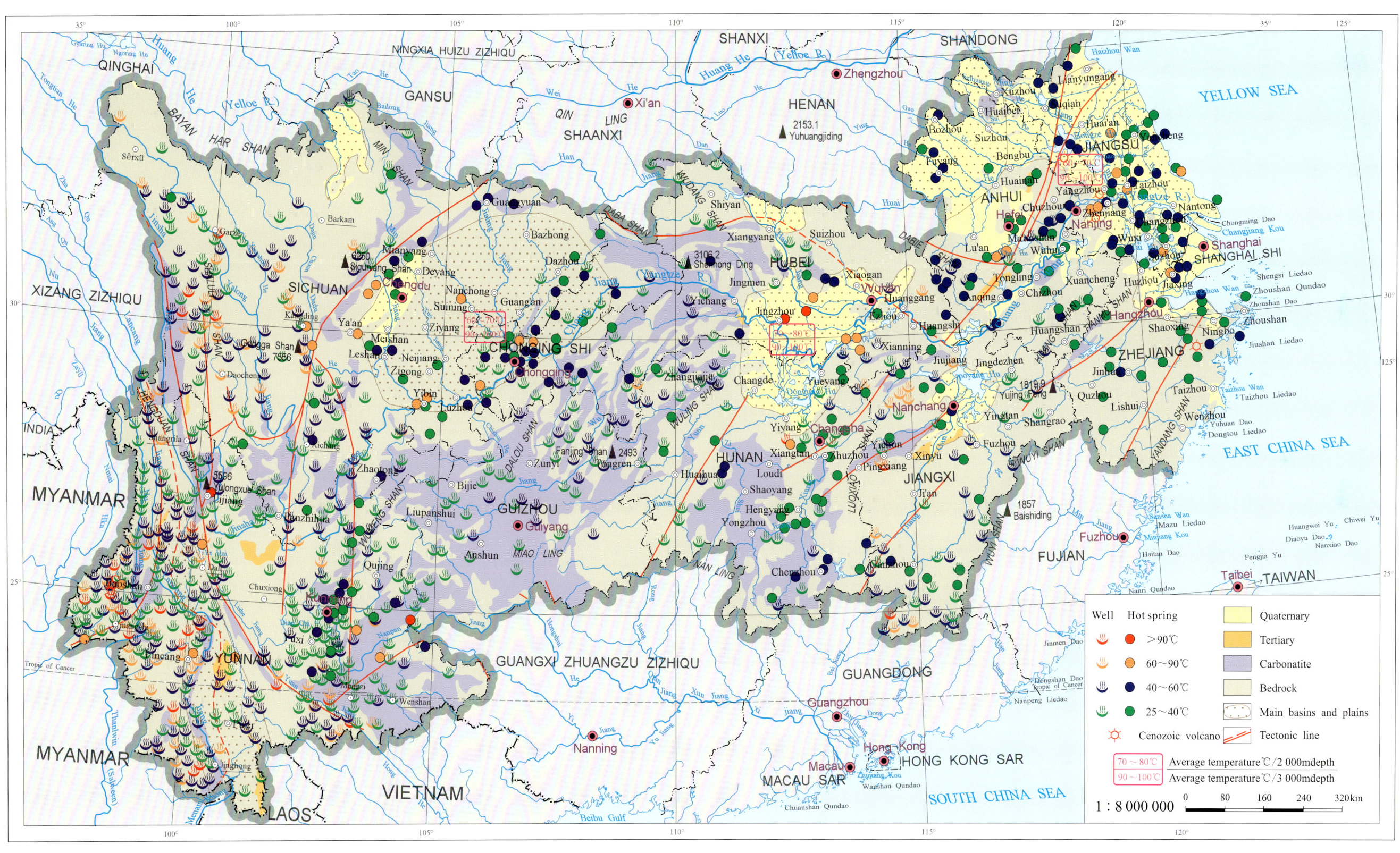

Figure 2 Geothermal resources in the YEZ

Figure 3 Active faults and earthquakes in the YEZ

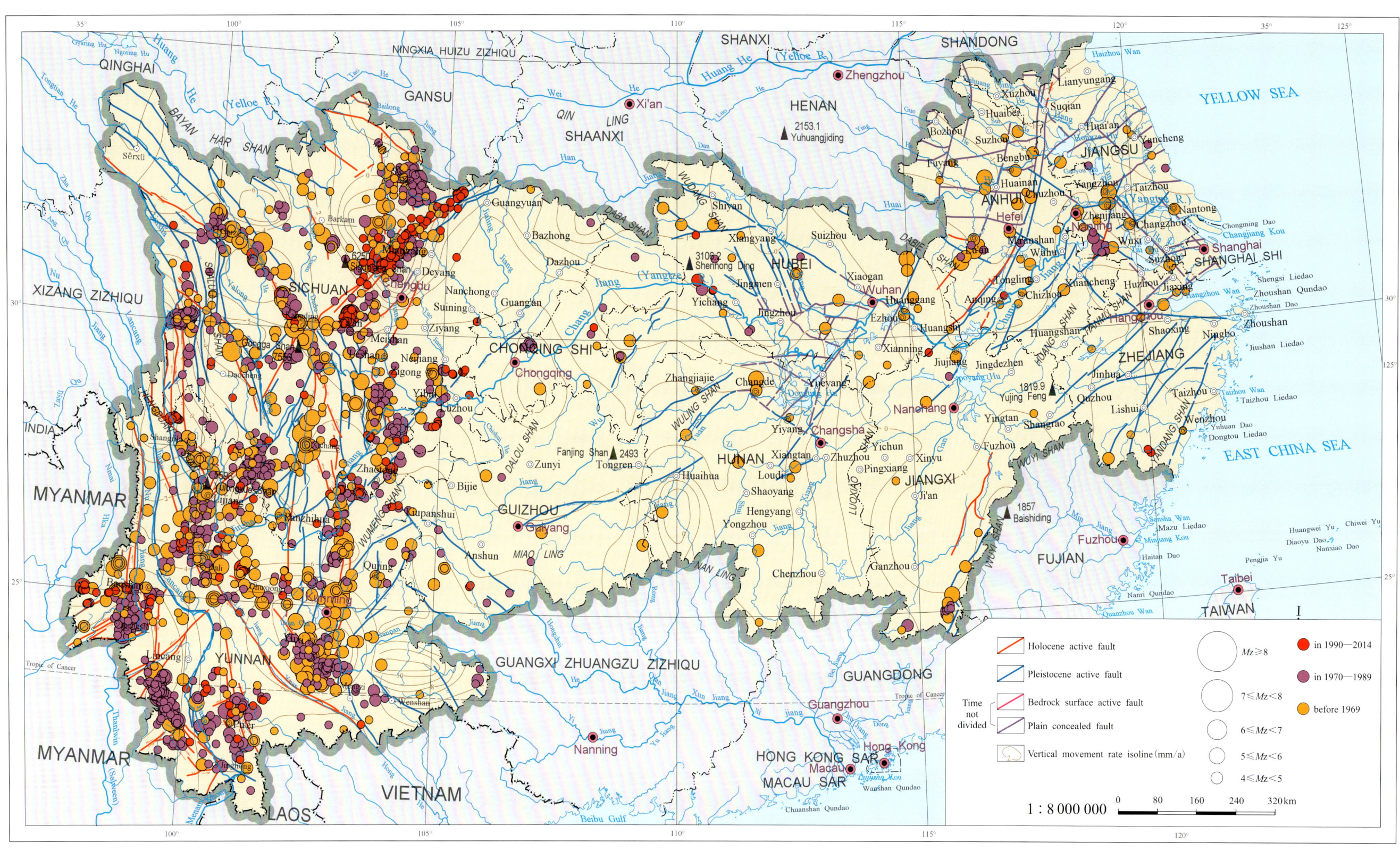

Figure 4 Karst collapse susceptibility assessment of the YEZ

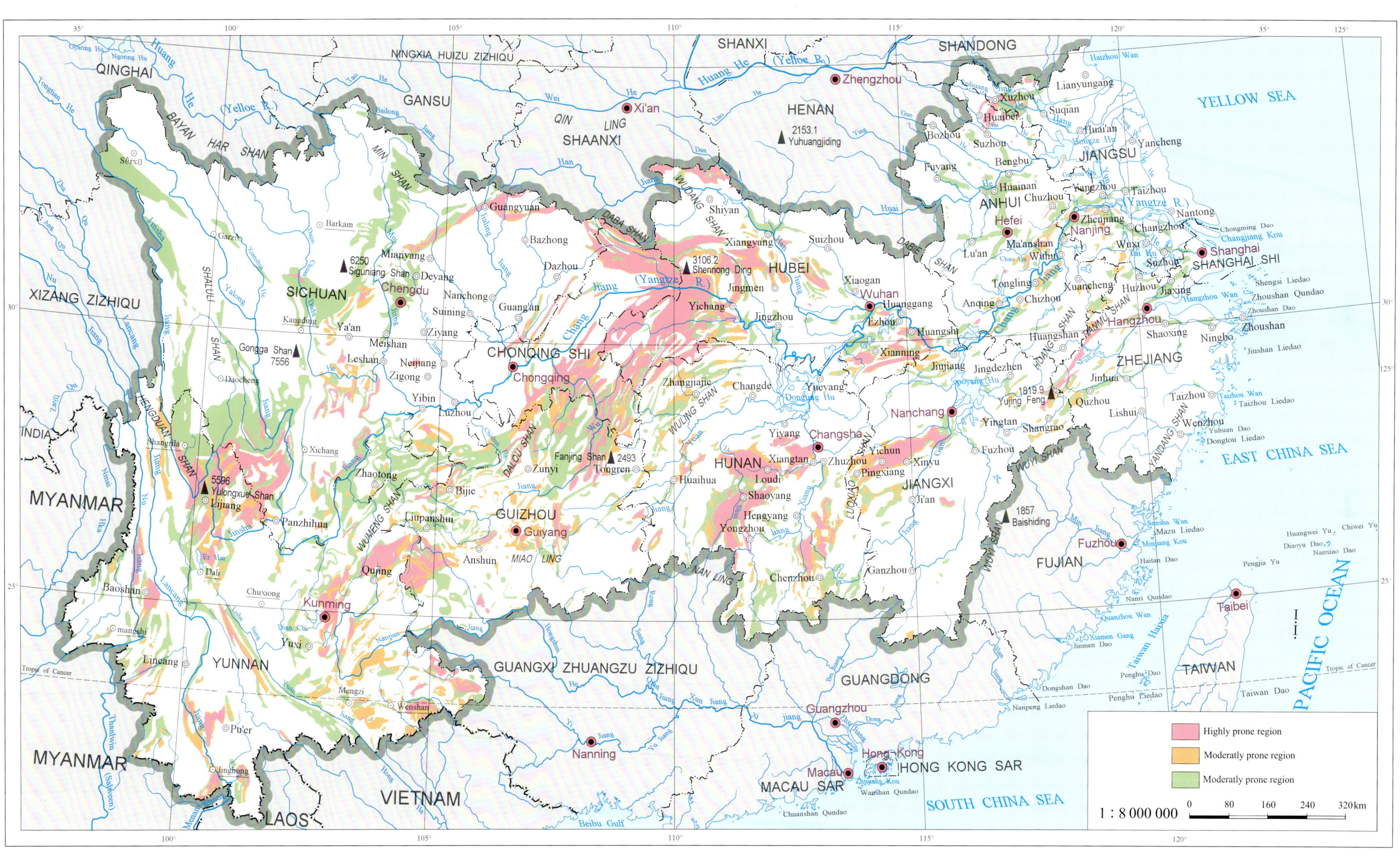

Figure 5 Landslide-rock fall-debris flows in the YEZ with susceptibility assessment

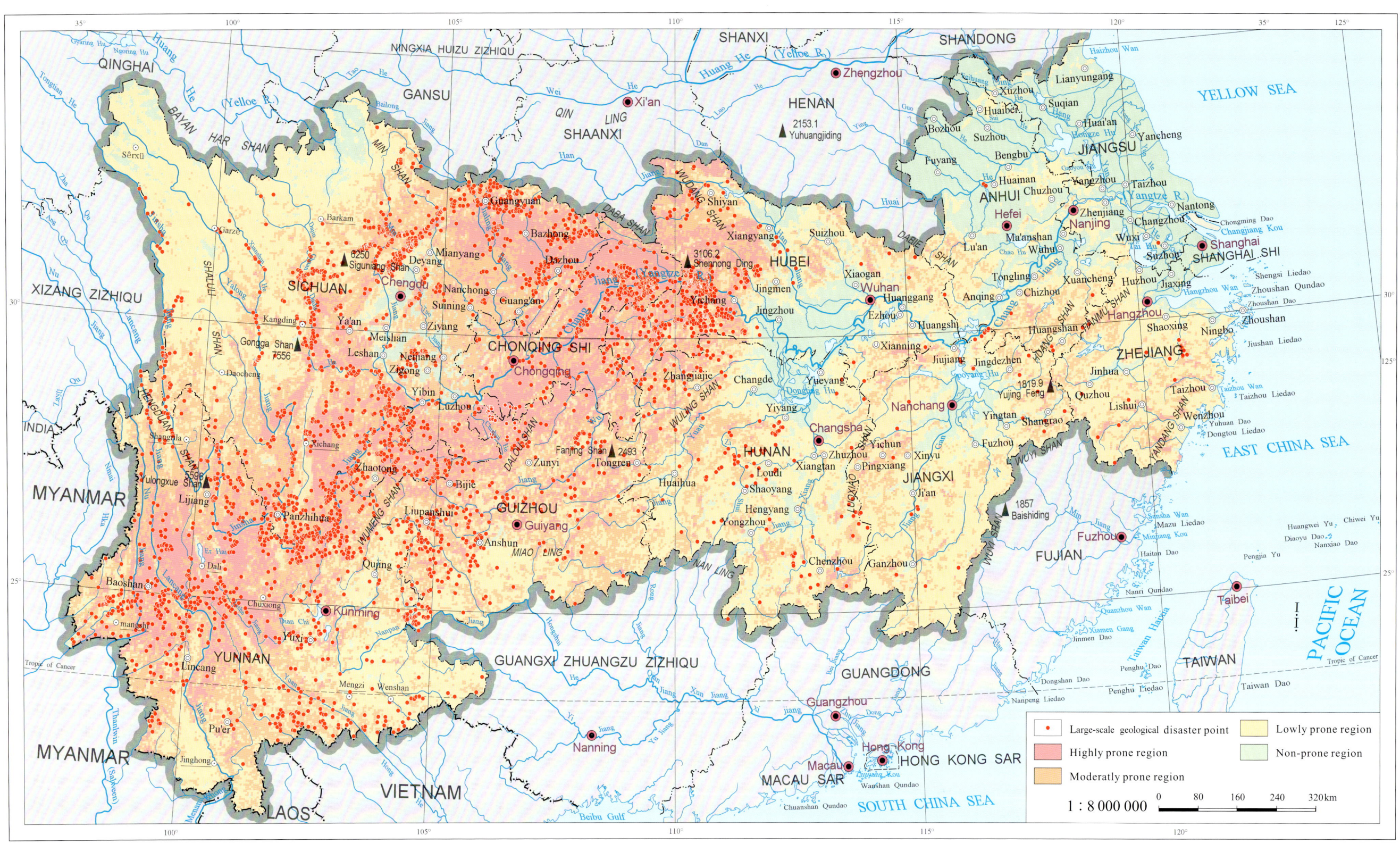

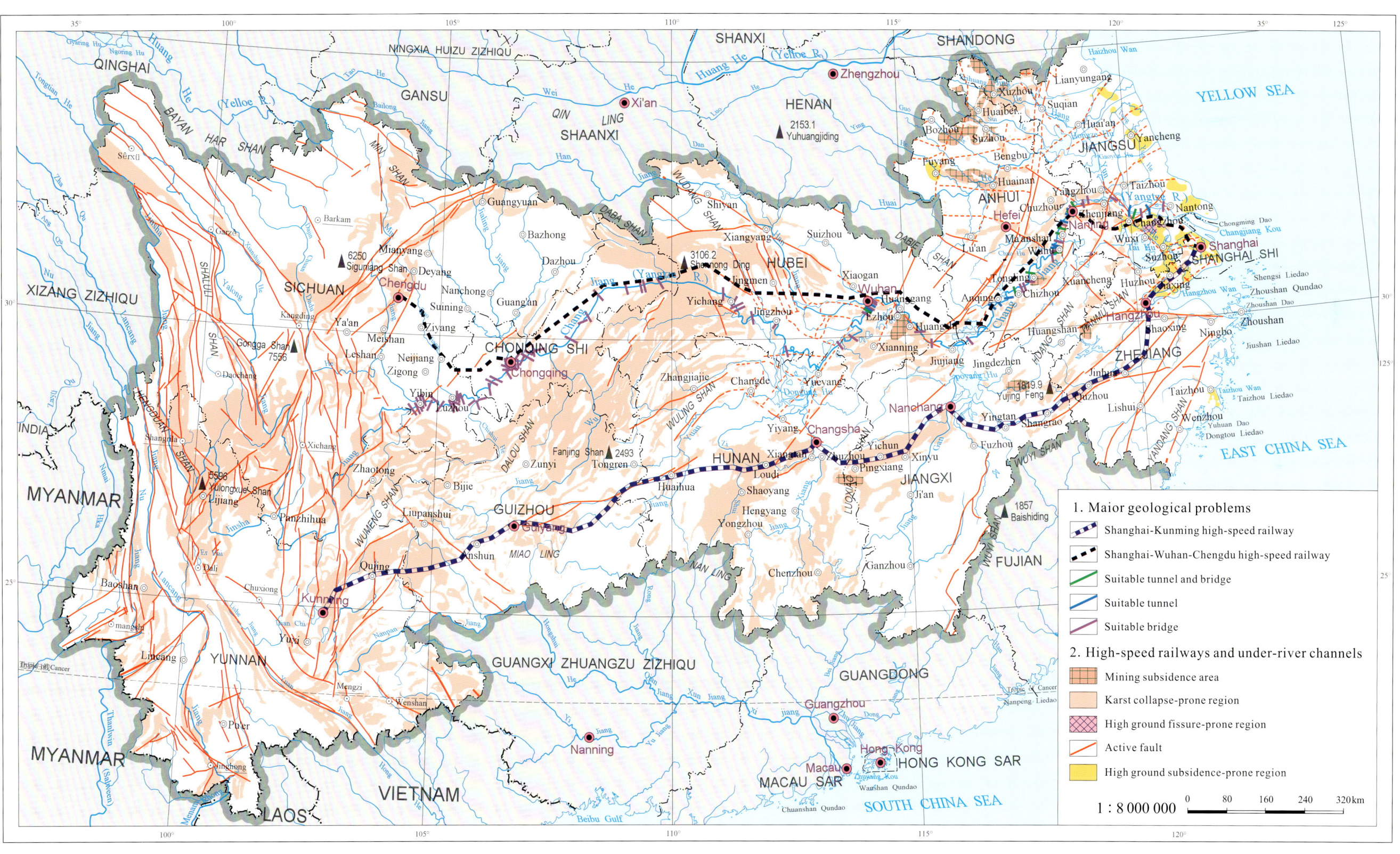

Figure 6　High-speed railways, river-crossing channels and momentous geological problems in the YEZ

Figure 7 The urban agglomerations and the main cities in the YEZ

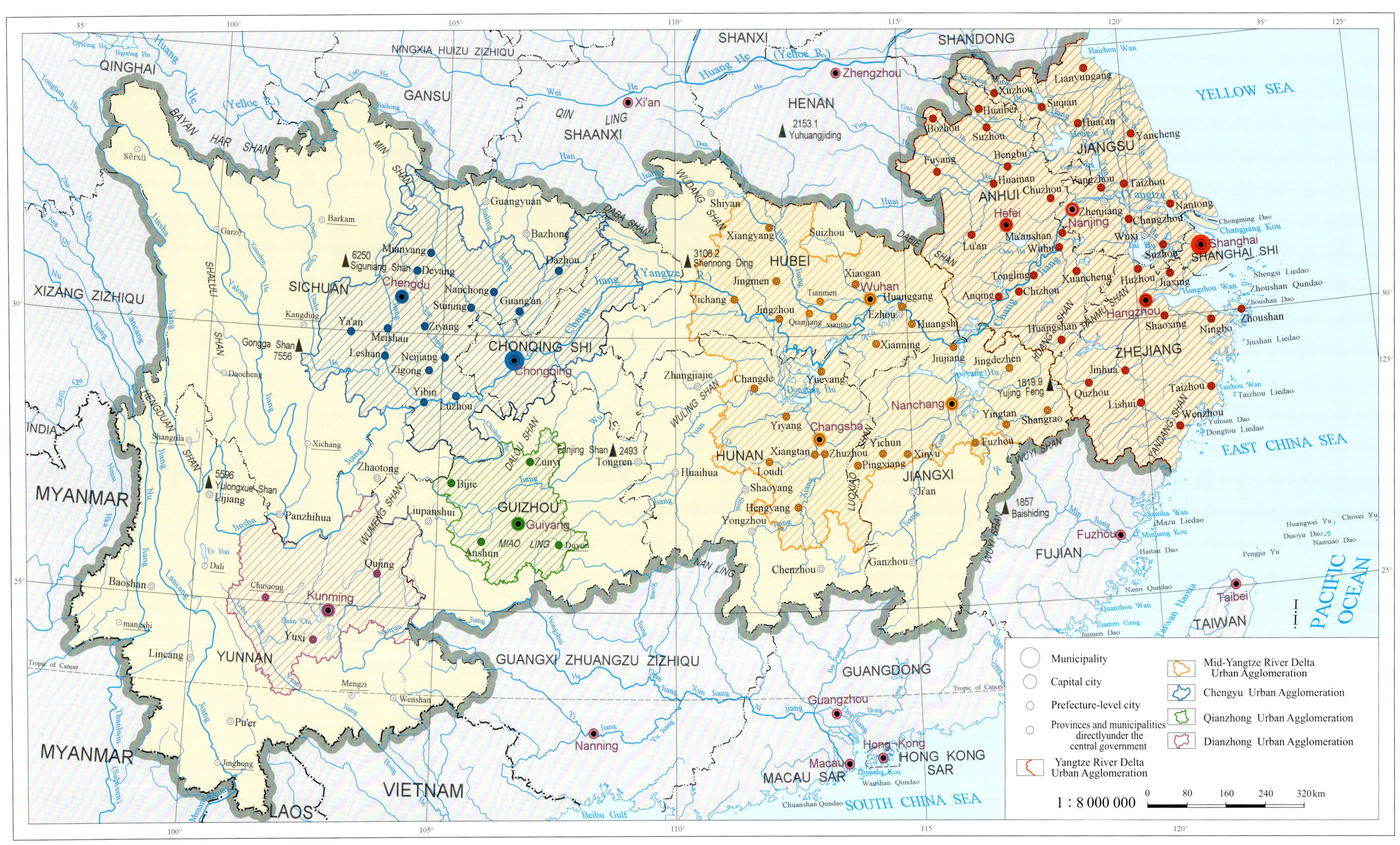

Figure 8 Large mineral resource bases in the YEZ

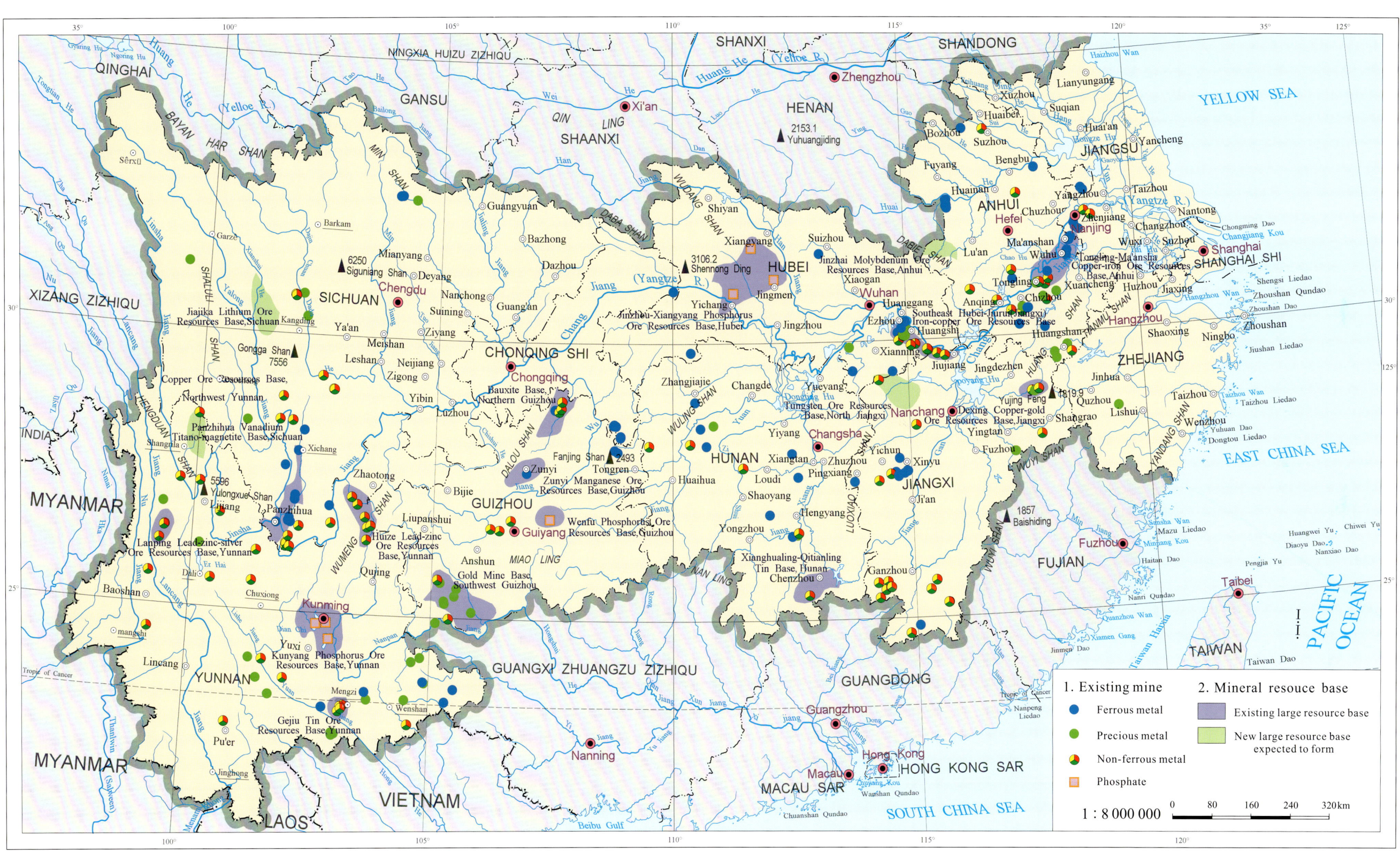

Table 1 Distribution of heavy metal-free arable land and green Se-rich arable land in the YEZ

Province/Municipality	Green Se-rich Arable Land($\times 10^4$mu)	Heavy Metal-free Arable Land($\times 10^4$mu)
Shanghai	6	736
Jiangsu	133	11,615
Zhejiang	347	2,654
Anhui	213	7,552
Jiangxi	325	3,339
Hubei	350	7,009
Hunan	256	2,240
Chongqing	43	2,719
Sichuan	142	7,027
Guizhou	18	48
Yunnan	3	310
Total	1,836	45,249

Table 2 Momentous geological problems in the river-crossing channels of the YEZ

Province	Location of Under-river Channel	Momentous Geological Problems	Recommended Control Measures
Jiangsu	Changtai	Wuxi-Suqian fault	Detailed investigation into active faults to further identify their location and activity. If an active fault passes through the planned location, this location would have to be re-adjusted or, if no re-adjustment is to be made, seismic mitigation measures should be taken and seismic monitoring maintained during the operation period
Jiangsu	Wufengshan	Wuxi-Suqian fault, Maoshan fault	
Jiangsu	Zhangjing	Jintan-Nandu fault	
Jiangsu	Shangyuanmen	Nanjing-Hushu fault	
Hubei	Wuxue	Xiangyang-Guangji fault, Tancheng-Lujiang fault	
Hubei	Qipanzhou	Xiangyang-Guangji fault	
Hubei	Ezhou-Huangshi II	Xiangyang-Guangji fault	
Sichuan	Mianyang-Suining-Neijing-Yibin Railway	Huayingshan fault	
Sichuan	Baitashan	Huayingshan fault	
Hubei	Wuhan Metroline 11	Karstcollapse	Detailed investigation into the karst geology of the buried karst regions to identify the exact location of the karst. If large karst caves are present in the planned location, the location of the bridge would have to be re-adjusted, if no re-adjustment is to be made, engineering treatment should be made and karst collapse or deformation monitoring maintained
Hubei	Jiayu	Karstcollapse	
Hubei	Chibi	Karstcollapse	

Table 3 Recommended method for the river-crossing channels in the YEZ

Location of River-crossing Channels	Selection Basis	Qty	Recommended Method
Honghuatao, Wujiagang, Yichangrail, Doushantuo in Hubei; Anzhangrailway, Fengjie, Anping, Guling, Wanzhouringexpressway, Xituo, Shunxi, Xingyi, Changshou III, Changshou II, Luoqi, Leijiapo, Guoyuan, Guojiatuo, southeastern ring of therailway, Xintian, Xintiangang railway, Huangjueping, Egongyan, Lijiatuo, Xiaonanhai, Hanjiatuo, Huangjuetuo, Baijusi, Wujutuo, Youxi and, Baisha in Chongqing; Rongshan, Hejiannew town, Hejiang county, Tai'an II, Shaxi, Lantian, Naxi, Anfu II, Anfu I, Jiang'an II, Nanxi, Luolong, Yanpingba, Mianyang-Suining-Neijiang-Yibinrailway, Baitashan, Jinsha River in Puheand Douba in Sichuan	Located in the upper reaches of theYangtzeRiver, where the riverbed is deeply cut and thickly overburdened with pebblegravel, which is not good for building tunnels. The bedrock is shallowly buried and theriverbankis steady, which is good for building bridges	48	Bridge
Xitong, Jiangyin II, Wufeng shan, Ningyi, Qixianghe, Shangyuanmen in Jiangsu; Cihu, Gushu, Yijishan II, Longwohu, Henggang, Meilong, Jiangkou, Haikou in Anhui; Susong in Anhui and Jiangxi; Wuxue, Qipanzhou, Ehuang II, WuhanLine 10, Qingshan, Yangsigang, Zhuankou, Jiayu, Chibi, Shishou, Jingzhou II and Zhijiang in Hubei	Located in the middle and lower reaches of the Yangtze River, where the riverbed is deeplycut, the rock mass is heterogeneous and the riverbed deposition thickness is small, which is not good for building tunnels. The maximum deepwater horizon is in themiddle, the watercourse is straight and the water surface and beaches are narrow, which is good for building bridges	27	Bridge
Zhangjing, Changtai, Nanjing Line 4, Nanjing V, Jinwen Road in Jiangsu; Taishan Road, Jiuhua Road, Chi'an, Anqing; Wuhan Metroline 7, Line 8 and Line 11 in Anhui	Located in the middle and lower reaches of the Yangtze River, where the maximum deep water horizon is close to the bank and thewater-frontis heavily eroded, which is not good for building bridges	12	Tunnel
Jiangyin III, Nanjing and Yan Road, Hanzhong West Road in Jiangsu; Ma'anshan Hubei Road, Longshan Road, South Wuhu, Tongling Development Zone, Chizhou in Anhui	Located in the middle and lower reaches oftheYangtze River, where the geological conditions are good for building tunnels and bridges	8	Bridge or tunnel

Table 4 Surface subsidence in the Yangtze River Delta Urban Agglomeration and the affected cities

Region	Area with Accumulated Subsidence Greater than 200mm (km²)	Affected Cities	Accumulated Max. Subsidence (mm)	AVG. Subsidence Rate (mm/a)
Shanghai	1,068.6	Downtown, Minhang,Pudong,Jiading, Baoshan, Qingpu & local place of Songjiang	2,980	5.2
Suzhou–Wuxi–Changzhou	5,240.2	Suzhou,Wujiang, Kunshan,Taicang, Changshu, Zhangjiagang,Wuxi, Jiangyin, Changzhou	2,800	4.4
Hangzhou–Jiaxing–Huzhou	3,545.7	Jiangxing, Haining,Pinghu,Tongxiang, Jiashan, Haiyan, Eastern Huzhou, Northern Hangzhou	1,097	6.9
Coastal area of Jiangsu	10,590.0	Yancheng, Dafeng, Funing, Sheyang, Binhai,Guannan,Xiangshui,Nantong	717	25.6

Table 5 Karst collapse in the Yangtze River Delta Urban Agglomeration and the affected cities

Karst Collapse Region	Area(km²)	Affected Cities
Wuhan, Huangshi–Ezhou, Xianning–Jiayu	2,027	Wuhan,Ezhou,Huangshi,Daye, Xianning, Jiayu, Chibi, Chongyang
Ruichang-Jiujiang–riversideareaof Pengze	440	Ruichang, Jiujiang, Hukou,Pengze
Pingxiang–Fengcheng–Leping	1,630	Luxi, Yichun, Fenyi, Xinyu,Shanggao,Gao'an,Zhangshu, Fengcheng,Yueping,Yiyang
Changsha–Zhuzhou–Xiangtan, Hunan province	320	Changsha Yuelu, Ningxiang,Xiangtan,Zhuzhou
Changde	229	Changde
Jingshan–Zhongxiang	55.3	Jingshan,Zhongxiang

Table 6 Main geological concerns in the Chengyu Urban Agglomeration and the affected cities

Cities at or above Prefectural Level	County/City/Prefecture	Geological Concern
Chengdu	Dujiangyan,Pengzhou	Earthquake
Deyang	Mianzhu,Shifang	Earthquake
Mianyang	Pingwu,Anxian	Earthquake
Ya'an	Yucheng, Mingshan, Yingjing, Hanyuan, Shimian, Tianquan, Lushan,Baoxing	Earthquake and the other geological disaster
Nanchong	Nanbu,Yilong	Geological disaster
Leshan	Jinhekou, Ebian,Mabian	Earthquake and the othere gological disaster
Luzhou	Xuyong,Gulin	Geological disaster
Neijiang	Neijiang	Geological disaster
Neijiang	Longchang	Earthquake
Yibin	Cuiping,Junlian, Gongxian, Xingwen,Pingshan	Geological disaster
Yibin	Changning, Gaoxian,Junlian	Earthquake
Zigong	Zigong	Geological disaster
Zigong	Zigong, Rongxian,Fushun	Earthquake
Chongqing	Zhongxian, Wanzhou, Yunyang,Fuling	Geological disaster

Table 7 Large mineral resource bases in the YEZ

Resource Base	Preserved Resource Reserve	Total Number of Mines
Tongling and Ma'anshan Cu-Fe resource base, Anhui	Cu: $96.4×10^4$t Fe: $6.7×10^8$t	90
Southeastern Hubei–Jiurui (Jiangxi) Fe-Cu base	Cu: $331.4×10^4$t Fe: $2.6×10^8$t	90
Jingzhou-Xiangyang P base, Hubei	P: $9.7×10^8$t	164
Xianghualing-Qitianling Sn base, Hunan	Sn: $5.1×10^4$t	51
Dexing Cu-Au base, Jiangxi	Cu: $552×10^5$t Au: 36.2t	23
Au base, southern Guizhou	Au: 126t	69
Wengfu P resource base, Guizhou	P: $2.1×10^8$t	19
Kunyang P resource base, Yunnan	P: $5.4×10^8$t	54
Zunyi Mn resource base, Guizhou	Mn: $249.5×10^4$ t	36
Bauxite base, northern Guizhou	Bauxite: $4,889×10^4$ t	16
Huize Pb-Zn resource base, Yunnan	Zn: $46.8×10^4$ t	9
Panzhihua V-Timagnetite base, Sichuan	Fe: $19.9×10^8$ t	159
Gejiu Sn resource base, Yunnan	Sn: $27.5×10^4$ t	11
Lanping Pb-Zn-Ag resource base, Yunnan	Pb: $46.8×10^4$t Zn: $640×10^4$t	17

后 记

图集中，地质矿产类图件（29张）由中国地质调查局负责组织编制，技术牵头单位为中国地质调查局南京地质调查中心，参加单位包括中国地质调查局武汉地质调查中心、中国地质调查局成都地质调查中心、中国地质环境监测院、中国地质调查局天津地质调查中心、中国地质调查局水文地质环境地质调查中心、中国地质科学院水文地质环境地质研究所、中国地质科学院岩溶地质研究所、中国地质科学院地质力学研究所、中国地质调查局青岛海洋地质研究所、中国地质科学院地质研究所、中国国土资源航空物探遥感中心、中国地质调查局发展研究中心、全国地质资料馆，以及江苏、浙江、上海、安徽、江西、湖北、湖南、四川、重庆、云南、贵州11个省（市）国土资源厅（局）、地质矿产勘查开发局、地质调查院、地质环境监测总站等。图集中，土地类图件（6张）由中国土地勘测规划院编制。